BLUEPRINTS
Distant Places

Joy A Palmer

Stanley Thornes (Publishers) Ltd

Do you receive BLUEPRINTS NEWS?

Blueprints is an expanding series of practical teacher's ideas books and photocopiable resources for use in primary schools. Books are available for separate infant and junior age ranges for every core and foundation subject, as well as for an ever widening range of other primary teaching needs. These include **Blueprints Primary English** books and **Blueprints Resource Banks**. **Blueprints** are carefully structured around the demands of National Curriculum in England and Wales, but are used successfully by schools and teachers in Scotland, Northern Ireland and elsewhere.

Blueprints provide :
- Total curriculum coverage
- Hundreds of practical ideas
- Books specifically for the age range you teach
- Flexible resources for the whole school or for individual teachers
- Excellent photocopiable sheets - ideal for assessment and children's work profiles
- Supreme value

Books may be bought by credit card over the telephone and information obtained on **(0242) 228485**. Alternatively, photocopy and return this **FREEPOST** form to receive Blueprints News, our regular update on all new and existing titles. You may also like to add the name of a friend who would be interested in being on the mailing list.

Please add my name to the **BLUEPRINTS NEWS** mailing list.

Mr/Mrs/Miss/Ms --

Home address ---

--Postcode -----------------------

School address ---

-- Postcode -----------------------

Please also send **BLUEPRINTS NEWS** to :

Mr/Mrs/Miss/Ms --

Address ---

-- Postcode -----------------------

To: Marketing Services Dept., Stanley Thornes Ltd, FREEPOST (GR 782), Cheltenham, GL50 1BR

Text © Joy Palmer 1994
Original line illustrations © ST(P) Ltd 1994

The right of Joy Palmer to be identified as author of this work has been asserted by her in accordance with the Copyright, designs and Patents Act 1988.

The copyright holders authorise ONLY users of **Blueprints** *Distant Places* to make photocopies or stencil duplicates of the copymasters for their own or their classes' immediate use within the teaching context.

No other rights are granted without permission in writing from the publishers or under licence from the Copyright Licensing Agency Limited. Further details of such licences (for reprographic reproduction) may be obtained from the Copyright Licensing Agency Limited, of 90 Tottenham Court Road, London W1P 9HE.

Copy by any other means or for any other purpose is strictly prohibited without the prior written consent of the copyright holders.

Applications for such permission should be addressed to the publishers.

First published in 1994 by:
Stanley Thornes (Publishers) Ltd
Ellenborough House
Wellington Street
CHELTENHAM GL50 1YD
England

A catalogue record for this book is available from the British Library.

ISBN 0–7487–1698–X

Typeset by Tech-Set, Gateshead, Tyne & Wear.
Printed in Great Britain by Beshara Press, Cheltenham

CONTENTS

Introduction		v
Distant Places:	Corfu	1
	Japan	20
	San Francisco Bay	39
	Hawaii	61
	New Zealand	81
	Brazil	100
	Egypt	117
Copymaster samples		**136**

INTRODUCTION

Blueprints *Distant Places* aims to provide a set of structured and comprehensive 'off-the-peg' resources for primary geography studies of places outside the UK. This is now a curriculum requirement in Scotland and Northern Ireland, as well as England and Wales, but it is often very difficult to obtain structured teaching materials for place studies. This book meets these needs.

In addition to its specific coverage of place study, this book also provides a huge resource of material for the development of a much wider range of geographical skills and knowledge which can be drawn on very flexibly. These areas include mapping skills and large parts of physical and human geography. You will find more specific details on the book's geography coverage and coverage of the curricula for England, Wales, Scotland and Northern Ireland below. Each study also has particularly strong links with history, and you will find history and geography highlighted on the webs.

Blueprints *Distant Places* consists of seven carefully chosen place studies.

These are:
- Corfu
- Japan
- San Francisco Bay
- Hawaii
- New Zealand
- Brazil
- Egypt

The selection of places has been made on two criteria: scale of place and location. Thus the place studies range in scale from cities to complete countries, and include widely differing global locations, both the developed and the underdeveloped world and most of the continents – a country in Asia, South America and Africa, a group of Pacific Islands, a major city in the USA, a Mediterranean island, a country in the South Pacific.

For each place there is:
- a planning web showing geography coverage and cross-curricula links
- a comprehensive illustrated bank of teacher's activities and essential background information on the place
- six copymasters, including a map of the place chosen.

Each place has a clear focus on geography, whilst providing an extensive range of activities relating to other areas of the curriculum. For each place, however, there is a clear focus on a limited number of other areas rather than a superficial attempt to cover the entire curriculum. This allows for each topic to be focused in geography, whilst making meaningful and in-depth links with appropriately related areas. A matrix is provided which shows the curriculum areas covered in each case study.

Most of the material in this book has been collected first hand from the place. It is therefore authentic and original. It provides you with resources that are simply unobtainable elsewhere and which are accurate and reliable. It is expected that the book will be most widely used with the 7–11 age range, but no attempt has been made to grade the suggested activities or to link them in a formal way to specific Key Stages or Levels of Attainment and much of the material can be successfully used with younger children. A great deal of emphasis is placed throughout the book on helpful background information for teachers. It is anticipated, therefore, that teachers will adapt much of the book's content into forms and tasks that are appropriate for their own pupils, at whatever stage of learning they may be.

The book is, however, intended to meet the relevant demands of all the UK primary geography curricula of which a brief outline follows.

Coverage of geography skills and content

You will find below reference to each specific UK primary geography curriculum, but here we offer a general outline of the book's coverage.

1. **Geography skills:** Each place study provides a map and a range of mapping activities which can be interpreted at successive levels depending on the age of the children.

2. **Study of places:** This is of course at the centre of the book's coverage. Each place study will give children a knowledge of the place and the distinctive features that create its identity, a sense of the place's interconnectedness with the rest of the world and an issues-based study related to the place (e.g. 'Tourism – Good or Bad?' in Corfu and 'The Great Burger Debate' in Brazil). The place studies allow children to get a very rounded idea of what 'makes' a place and include a study of its history, culture, climate, landscape, daily life, plants and animals.

3. **Physical geography:** Particular coverage is given to key features of physical geography and includes:
   - weather and climate (every place study covers this)
   - rivers and seas (a strong feature of the studies of San Francisco and Brazil)
   - landforms
   - animals, plants and soils.

4. **Human geography:** You will find the human dimension of geography strongly represented. This includes population issues, study of settlement, transport and communications, and economic activities.

One of the strengths of the studies is that they can be used comparatively. You could, for example, choose to compare and contrast housing or tourism in two different places.

Curriculum coverage

Geography in the National Curriculum (England and Wales)

The studies can be used widely across all the ATs (Geographical Skills, Knowledge and Understanding of

v

Places, Physical Geography, Human Geography) as outlined in the previous section. They will directly resource the Programmes of Study for Knowledge and Understanding of Places in detail as follows:

At **Key Stage 1** children are asked specifically to study a locality beyond the United Kingdom. Corfu may be one which a few infant children will have visited on holiday; alternatively New Zealand may provide the possibility of links with relatives, school twinning and the study of a place culturally linked to the one children know.

At **Key Stage 2** children are asked to study a locality in an economically developing country and one within the EEC. Brazil would make an excellent study for the first and Corfu for the second.

The Northern Ireland Curriculum
The studies will richly resource all the ATs and there is much scope for geographical enquiry. The successive ATs 2–4 (Physical Environments, Human Environments, Place and Space) are all addressed in each study. You will find specific opportunities to study AT5 (Issues in a Changing World) as follows: tourism in Corfu; the fishing industry in Japan; threatened environments in San Francisco; the plight of the Maori people in New Zealand; the rain forest in Brazil.

The book will directly resource the Programmes of Study for AT4 (Place and Space) as follows:

At **Key Stage 1** children have to develop an awareness of place in a global context; specifically they also have to find out about places in the economically developing world to contrast with Northern Ireland. You might want to contrast Belfast with another city (San Francisco or Tokyo); you might want to contrast a Northern Irish farming community with life in the rain forest. All the place studies will make striking contrasts in climate, landscape, and weather and work.

At **Key Stage 2** children need to study physical, rural and urban features, more specifically to study Europe and the wider world. Corfu will make an excellent European study; any of the others will provide excellent material on the wider world. They will all allow children to compare and contrast with Northern Ireland the physical and human character of places, features which illustrate differences between places, and relationships between human and physical elements of landscapes.

Scotland: National Guides for Environmental Studies 5–14
Blueprints *Distant Places* will provide a rich resource for the social subjects dimension of Understanding People and Place and for the related Attainment Target strands.

The book will directly resource features of Understanding People and Place as follows:

At stages P1 to P3 the material will be valuable in introducing children to a wide range of geographical concepts relating to differences between places studied and their own locality. These include weather and physical climate, the relationship between people and places, children in other lands, transport and communications, and the use of maps.

At stages P4 to P6 the material will again be invaluable for studies of physical and human geography. Corfu will provide a comparative study within Europe; and case study material can be used from across the place studies to examine a particular element of People and Place. This could be housing, climate, holidays, work or communications. At the back of the book you will find information and two photocopiable sheets from the Blueprints Geography Resource Banks which contain useful distant places resources to use alongside this book.

Matrix to show principal location of topics in subject areas of the National Curriculum

Topic	Geography	History	English/Drama	Mathematics	Science/Technology	Art	Music	PE	RE	Environmental Education
Corfu	●	●	●		●	●	●		★	
Japan	●	●	●		●	●		●	●	●
San Francisco Bay	●	●	●		●	●			●	●
Hawaii	●	●	●	●		●	●	●	★	●
New Zealand	●	●	●		●	●				
Brazil	●	●		●	●	●	●			●
Egypt	●	●	●	●	●	●			●	

★ NOTE: Whilst RE is not identified as a separate area of study in these two topics, it is well reflected in their general content.

CORFU

Science
- Plant and animal life in Corfu
- Edible plants of Corfu
- Food of the island — design a menu

Geography
- Locate the Ionian Islands on a world map
- The six islands of the Heptanissa
- Shape and size of Corfu
- Physical geography — the Dinaric Alps
- Make an illustrated map of Corfu
- Climate of the island
- The tourist industry
- Plan a holiday in Corfu
- The indigenous way of life
- Yearly pattern — holidays and festivals
- Make a Corfu calendar

Music
- Traditional music of the island
- Folk dances
- Traditional musical instruments

CORFU cross-curricular links

History
- Time line of Corfu's history
- Evidence of prehistoric times
- Temple of Artemis
- Legend of nymph Kerkira
- Homer's *Odyssey*
- Greek myths and legends
- Key characters in the island's history
- The ten ages of Corfu
- Historic Corfu Town
- Desire for independence

English
- The various names for Corfu
- Learn some Greek
- Famous writers of Corfu
- Debate: 'Tourism — Good or Bad?'
- Travel excursions

Art and architecture
- Famous buildings of the island
- Icons and art
- Corfu townscape
- Construct a rural house
- Corfu scenes with views out to sea

Corfu

INTRODUCTION

The Greek island of Corfu (*Kerkyra* in Greek) is one of the Ionian Islands, set in the Ionian Sea off the north-west coast of Greece. As the Ionian Islands have a common history, the group will be discussed as a whole at various points throughout this topic, notably in the activities on geography and history (pages 2–9). A wide range of other activities, set in the context of appropriate background material, will focus on the island of *Kerkyra* itself.

The Ionian Islands are often referred to as 'The Riviera of Greece'. With their hot, usually rain-free summers, the islands provide an ideal setting for tourism, especially as the surrounding sea and prevailing winds prevent them from having the very extreme heat often endured on mainland Greece. Corfu experiences more winter rain than many of the other Greek islands, which results in rich vegetation. It has an exciting mixed landscape of sea-shore and mountains, fertile plains and rich natural vegetation.

Corfu has a remarkably interesting history, further details of which are provided on pages 6–7, beginning with the arrival of colonists from Eretria (a city of Euboea) in about 700 BC. The island has many fascinating and diverse claims to fame: Corfu is thought by many to be the island of Scheria that is portrayed in Homer's *Odyssey* as the home of the Phaeacian and their King, Alcinous; the nineteenth-century author Edward Lear lived there, as did the well-known twentieth-century wildlife author Gerald Durrell; Corfu is also the birthplace of HRH The Duke of Edinburgh.

Some 90 000 people now permanently inhabit the island of Corfu, 35 per cent of whom live in Corfu Town.

GEOGRAPHY

Activity 1: Where is Corfu?
Begin by discussing the physical setting of the Ionian Islands and their names. **Copymaster 1** (The Ionian Islands) provides a basis for this activity. Use the copymaster alongside a globe or map of the world so that the children can locate the Ionian Sea in the eastern Mediterranean region and appreciate the proximity of the islands to mainland Greece.

Suggest that the islands and mainland are coloured (with Albania in a different colour). The map can then be annotated at this or any later stage in the topic by adding, for example, the location of key towns, a scale, and approximate distances. The following information may be helpful.

Background information
There are some 320 kilometres (200 miles) between the most northerly and southerly tips of the Ionian Islands. Corfu's north-eastern corner is only 5 kilometres (3 miles) from the coast of Albania. Italy is some 100 kilometres (62 miles) from Corfu's north-western coast. Corfu is in the north of the Ionian Sea at the entrance to the Adriatic.

Only the major islands in this group have been drawn and labelled. Perhaps smaller ones could be located and added, such as *Antipaxi, Othoni, Erikoussa,* and *Mathraki*.

Activity 2: The Ionian Islands
Early in the topic it will be necessary to explain the number of main islands in this group. The map on Copymaster 1 shows six, these being Corfu, Paxoi, Lefkada, Ithaka, Cephalonia and Zakynthos. (Note that here the English names are used, whereas the copymaster shows the Greek names. Depending on the age of the children, decide which will be your focus. The words Corfu and *Kerkyra* are used interchangeably throughout this text, and other names for the island are also introduced in the history and English activities.

Obviously, this variety of terminology will need clarification at the outset.) However, although the map has six islands, the Greeks call the group the *Heptanissa* meaning 'the seven islands'. This phrase will be used within the history section of the topic, so you should explain that the administration of the islands at one time also included the island of Kithera, even though it is some distance away, off the south-eastern coast of the Peloponnese.

Activity 3: The island of Corfu
Use **Copymaster 2** (*Kerkyra*), as a basis for discussion of the shape and size of the island of Corfu. Its total area is 595 square kilometres and it is second in size to Cephalonia (780 square kilometres) in the Ionian group. Corfu is only 65 kilometres (40 miles) from north to south, stretching some 25 kilometres (16 miles) across the top and then tapering sharply down to a long, narrow curve. The shape of the island as a whole resembles a blade, and ancient sources call the island *Drepanon* meaning 'sickle'. It has also been suggested that Corfu looks like a smaller image of Italy.

Corfu is famous today for its beaches, yet it is a mountainous island. The outlines of the main mountain areas are shown on the copymaster. Mountains could be coloured brown by the children and, if appropriate, more detail could be included.

Background information
Corfu has a mountainous spine. The highest peak on the island is Pantokrator in the northern bulge, which reaches a height of 910 metres. Another well-known peak is Ayii Dheka (550 metres), south-west of Corfu Town. The individual islands in the group are essentially the peaks and plateaus of a mountain range that extends down from the former Yugoslavia and Albania, forming the western part of Greece and then re-emerging as Crete. Geologists call this range the Dinaric Alps, which are an extension of the main European Alps.

Activity 4: Features of the island

Copymaster 2 has been left blank deliberately, so that it can be used in a variety of ways. The map below has been annotated with the mountain peaks mentioned and also shows Corfu's main tourist centres. This is background information to which the children could have access when annotating their own maps. Perhaps an enlarged map of the island could be drawn and used as the centre of a wall display, with 'picture postcard' style paintings around it at appropriate points, as on the artwork below, to show some of the main features and attractions of Corfu. Some suggestions for these are given below. Completion of this major display could be an on-going concern throughout the topic, as various aspects of the island's history and culture unfold. The children's own copymasters could be used to record places, before they are transferred to the class display.

Background information

Possible features and attractions to highlight on the map might include:

- mountain peaks (e.g. Pantokrator, Ayii Dheka)
- beaches (e.g. Sidari, Kavos, Benitses, Acharavi, St Spiridon, Ag Georgios, Glyphada)
- tourist towns (e.g. Corfu Town, Kavos, Benitses, Kassiopi, Roda, Sidari, Paleokastritsa, Kanoni, Glyphada).

These are but a few of the main sites. Tourist brochures featuring Corfu can be obtained from travel agencies and will provide a splendid source of information about the island.

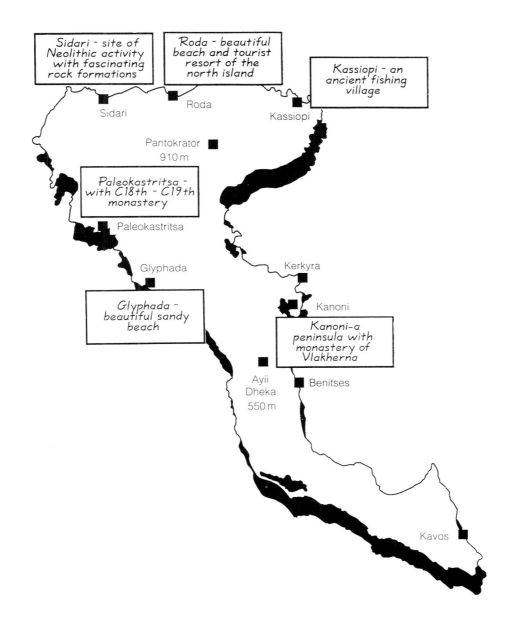

Corfu

Activity 5: The climate of Corfu
Discuss the climate of Corfu, one of the island's major attractions for summer tourists. Corfu has a typical Mediterranean climate of warm, wet winters and hot, dry summers. Rain generally falls between November and March, and the rest of the year is relatively dry, although thunderstorms often occur in late August and September, accompanied by strong winds. Because of the surrounding sea, the island escapes the intense and prolonged heat of the summer months as experienced by mainland Greece. The sea also has the effect of insulating the island during the winter months, so that temperatures do not fall as low as on the mainland. Compare temperature statistics of Greece and Britain by looking at records printed in daily newspapers: London and Athens will usually be shown in world temperature tables.

Activity 6: Tourism in Corfu

A Consider the tourist industry in Corfu, since it has been suggested that this island invented tourism! Let the children outline reasons why so many people visit the island each year. These could include:

- beautiful sandy beaches
- long, hot, sunny summers
- a fascinating history, with many places and buildings worth visiting
- friendly and hospitable local people
- hotels, apartments and *tavernas* (restaurants) providing excellent food and accommodation.

It could well be the case that one or more members of your class have visited Corfu on holiday. Ask them to talk about their experiences (where they stayed, what they did, what they ate, etc.) and bring in some of their holiday photographs or souvenirs, if possible.

B Plan an imaginary holiday in Corfu. This can be a very substantial activity which occupies the whole class, with pupils divided into groups to research various aspects of the holiday. Perhaps one group could be the travel agents who find out how to get there and where to stay (requiring investigation into timetables of flights from your nearest UK airport). Another group could be the financial advisers, who cost the holiday (using travel agency brochures to ascertain basic costings, then adding on estimated amounts for food, drink, travel and miscellaneous items such as sun-bed hire, sun cream, souvenirs, etc.). A final group could be responsible for advising the class on practicalities such as:

- places to go and see — pupils should/could write a tourist guide to the island, based on information gleaned from travel brochures and books
- documentation — pupils should/could issue a statement on passports, visas and customs control, currency exchange, etc.
- living in Corfu — pupils should/could give basic information about post offices, telephones, medical matters, money, personal services, etc.

This group could well be sub-divided, in order to research the topics adequately. The following information will help pupils with their inquiries.

Documentation
Visitors to Greece must have a valid national passport; in the case of European visitors, a European passport is acceptable. No visa is required for British citizens. Every visitor entering Greece passes through customs control — and unlimited amounts of traveller's cheques and currency (drachmas) may be taken into the country. Your local bank should be able to advise on exchange rates — and indeed, the whole concept of currency exchange rates might make an interesting sub-topic for the group to pursue, if time permits. A visit from a local bank manager for a structured interview would be valuable, if it can be arranged.

Living in Corfu
Post Offices are generally open from 8 a.m. to 2 p.m., although some close in the middle of the day. Postage stamps can usually be bought in hotels, kiosks and mini-markets. Telephone kiosks or *periptera* are found in town squares, and in hotels and shops in more remote places. Some are pay phones (you need a lot of change in drachma coins for a long-distance call) and some are metered. Alternatively, you can visit the local office of the national phone company (OTE), open between 8 a.m. and 4 p.m., make the call from there and then pay the bill, which is based on the metered number of units your call has used.

With regard to medical matters, the local pharmacy is extremely helpful in dealing with minor illnesses or problems such as sunburn, upset tummy or mosquito bites. Many remedies are available over the counter. For anything more serious, tourist towns and villages always have a physician on call 24 hours a day. In an emergency, tourists can contact either the Tourist Police of Greece (tel. 30265) or the local police (tel. 100). Potential tourists should be reminded to take out full medical and baggage insurance (the financial team should be dealing with this!).

The unit of currency is the drachma, which comes in coins of 1, 2, 5, 10, 20, 50 and 100 drachmas, and notes of 100, 500, 1000 and 5000 drachmas. Banks are usually open from 8 a.m. until 2 p.m. from Monday to Friday. Hotels and tourist exchanges are open seven days a week in popular tourist areas and will change currency and traveller's cheques, while major credit cards can be used to withdraw cash.

Greece uses an A(lternative) C(urrent) of 220 volts, and, therefore, adaptors are needed for electrical appliances. Potential tourists should be advised to buy a universal plug. Greek television is heavily dependent on programmes purchased from British and American TV companies. Many *tavernas* and cafes have public television sets, often tuned to sporting events such as football and basketball. Greek radio broadcasts news bulletins in English, French, German and Arabic. BBC and European radio stations can be picked up on a short-wave radio. Thanks to tourism, English newspapers can be easily purchased — at great cost!

Potential tourists should be warned about Corfu plumbing, which is very primitive. Pipes will easily become blocked, so toilet paper should be placed in the appropriate bin beside the toilet, *not* flushed down it.

Finally, tourists should not drink Corfu tap water, as this can cause stomach upsets because of its high mineral content. Bottled water should be bought for drinking and cleaning teeth — it is very inexpensive.

C Compile as much information as possible into a 'Tourist Guide' booklet, or write it out on a wall display. A good role-play activity for children is to set up a small travel agent's corner in the classroom, to which they can go to book their Greek holiday and find out all about the attractions of places such as Corfu.

Activity 7: The native way of life in Corfu

A Find out more about the way of life of the indigenous people of Corfu, the Corfiots. Whilst very many are involved in the tourist trade, others lead a quiet, tranquil, rural existence. Farming and fishing are common occupations, as people are obliged to find their own food from the land or sea.

B Discuss the primitive nature of life in Corfu in comparison to that in most parts of the UK. Suggest that children write accounts of daily life in rural Corfu and mention, for example, that goats, donkeys, sheep, pigs and hens are frequently kept, wool is spun to make garments, and vegetables and fruit are grown at home. (Link this exercise with the science activities on plants of Corfu on page 11, and Copymaster 6 on making a typical rural house on page 19.)

Activity 8: The pattern of life in Corfu

A Investigate the yearly pattern of life in Corfu, by identifying and describing national holidays and festivals that are celebrated.

Background information
There are four major festivals associated with the island's patron saint, Spyridon. These are:

- Palm Sunday, when the anniversary of Corfu's deliverance from the plague in 1629 is celebrated
- the Saturday before Easter Sunday, commemorating the occasion in the sixteenth century when St Spyridon intervened to save the island from a terrible famine. The story tells how boats which had been trading elsewhere arrived unexpectedly in Corfu, carrying the meat which helped to save the islanders from starvation
- 11 August, a feast in memory of events during the Turkish siege of Corfu, when St Spyridon was said to have dressed as a monk and gone with angels in pursuit of the enemy, carrying a lighted candle in one hand and the Holy Cross in the other
- the first Sunday in November, called Litany Day and established by the Venetians in 1673. On this day the islanders remember how Spyridon again intervened to save Corfu from cholera.

Key national holidays include 1 January (New Year's Day), 6 January (Epiphany), the last Monday before Lent, Good Friday, Easter Sunday and Easter Monday, 25 March (Greek Independence Day), May Day (1 May), 15 August (Assumption of the Virgin Mary), 28 October (Okhi Day) and 25 December (Christmas Day).

B Suggest that children paint or make collage pictures of local people in the traditional costume worn on feast days.

Corfiots in traditional costume

C Make a Corfu calendar with a page for each month, suitable drawings or paintings, and the feast days and holidays mentioned above highlighted. This could be done as an individual or class activity, in which small groups work on a page for each month.

HISTORY

Activity 9: The history of Corfu

The history of Corfu and indeed of the Ionian Islands is long and complex. It is suggested that this topic could lead to a very significant linking between the curriculum areas of geography and history at Key Stage 2. Within the current constraints of space, an overview of Corfu's history is provided which allows substantial scope for further research and investigation of the key historical periods referred to. In the first instance, why not make a wall display of writing and illustrations, or a class book outlining the key periods and events in Corfu's history? The following background information is in itself, however, sufficient to complete a very worthwhile sub-topic on the history of the Ionian Islands.

Corfu

Background information

Neolithic pottery and other artefacts have been found on the island of Corfu, though no solid evidence of settlements during this period remains. In the Bronze Age, Corfu was described in Homer's *Odyssey* as the rich island of the Phaeacians, ruled by King Alcinous, whose daughter Nausicaa found Odysseus wading ashore from his wrecked ship.

The true history of Corfu, or Corcyra as it was then known, began with the arrival of colonists from Eretria, a city of Euboea around 700–775 BC. Shortly after this (664 BC), the earliest known sea battle involving Greek forces took place. Kypselos, the ruler of the Corinthians, tried to bring Corcyra under his control, but he was defeated by the Corfiots. Soon afterwards, however, they allied themselves with the Corinthians in a campaign to assist the Syracusans of Sicily in their fight against the tyrant of Gelas, Hipocrates. It should be noted that Corcyra, at this time, had one of the most significant fleets in the known world. Corcyra prospered, until eventually she began to resent the influence of Corinth and the two nations quarrelled (435 BC). Athens speedily came to the defence of Corcyra, thereby precipitating what became known as the Peloponnesian War (431–404 BC). During this war, the Athenians assembled a great armada at Corcyra in 415 BC and sailed off to Syracuse, which resulted in a disastrous defeat.

The Peloponnesian War is generally regarded as a conflict between Athens and Sparta, yet the pro-Athenian and pro-Spartan elements within Corcyra fought each other relentlessly for almost a century, while the real power in the region lay with Rome. Soon, the Romans were ruling the Ionian Islands, along with virtually all the ancient Greek domains. Several of the 'great' Romans, including Cato, Cicero and Nero visited Corcyra, and it was there that Octavius assembled his fleet in 31 BC before engaging Antony in battle further down the coast, off Actium.

During the times of Roman rule, the Ionian Islands were left very much to themselves: the Corfiots were granted complete autonomy over the island, and the Romans respected all of the island's ancient privileges. Then in AD 336, the Ionian Islands became part of the Eastern Roman Empire — the Byzantine Period. At this time, and particularly during the sixth century, Corcyra was open to countless attacks and invasions by pirates and other barbarian hordes intent upon plunder and destruction. During the so-called 'long, dark ages', the Gothic armies of Italy, the Saracens and other marauders of the Mediterranean continued to wreak havoc. Then in 1081, Normans under the son of Robert Guiscard (1015–1085), an adventurer, invaded and conquered Corcyra and other Ionian Islands. The Normans wanted the island as a base from which to penetrate eastwards. The Corfiots fought with grim determination, but Guiscard deployed his entire navy against the island and won the resulting battle.

The Crusades of the Middle Ages terrorised the island in the same way as the pirates of previous centuries had. While the island was still under Norman rule, various hordes of Crusaders crossed over to Corcyra from ports such as Pisa and Genoa, plundering the locality before returning to Italy once more. Then, after the Western Europeans of the Fourth Crusade took control of Constantinople and its empire in 1204, Corfu became one of the spoils that was fought over by the Venetians, the Genoese, the Angevin French and other warring factions. In 1386 the Venetians gained control of Corfu and ruled there for over 400 years.

This period of Venetian control was critical in terms of extending the Italian influence to the Ionian Islands. It was a time of intermingling between the two peoples, their languages, their cultures and artistic styles. Hence, there is an obvious Italian presence in both the landscape and the built environment of Corfu today. This also explains why the Italian dictator Benito Mussolini was determined to 'regain' the islands during the Second World War, as we shall discover later in this topic. The Venetian influence was powerful, yet the Corfiots retained their Greek language and Greek orthodox religion.

In 1797 Napoleon Bonaparte took control of Venice, and in turn France undertook responsibility for the governing of Corfu. This situation was welcomed by the islanders who believed that the 'free French spirit' of the recent revolution would inspire Bonaparte to extend that freedom to the Greeks too. However, at this time the great powers of Britain, Russia and Turkey did not approve of the French occupation of Corfu: indeed, between 1799 and 1807, a Turko-Russian force fought to remove the French from Corfu. On 21 March 1800, Russia and Turkey signed a treaty which effectively formed the islands into the *Heptanissa*, a seven-island state which was recognised by the great powers of Europe. The *Heptanissa* existed until 1807 when the Treaty of Tilsit, signed by Napoleon and Alexander I of Russia, caused the islands once again to come under French rule.

With the defeat of Napoleon, the Ionian Islands were claimed by Great Britain and also by Austria. The resolution of this divided interest lay with the influence of Count John Capodistrias, the Corfiot viceroy of the Russian Tsar. As a result of the viceroy's negotiations, the Treaty of Paris was signed in 1815 by Great Britain, Russia, Austria and Prussia. According to this agreement, the Ionian Islands were to be a free and independent state, that would come under the protection of Great Britain. The state was renamed 'The United States of the Ionian Islands', and in effect it was a colony of the British Empire. A Lord High Commissioner was to represent the King of Britain on the Islands. The first such Commissioner was Sir Thomas Maitland, appointed in 1816. Maitland's rule was harsh in its application and, whilst Britain introduced many improvements to Corfu, the Corfiots were still eager to obtain their freedom. A period of unrest followed, and many Corfiots joined a secret patriotic organisation known as the Society of Friends which dedicated itself to the struggle for Greek freedom.

Sir Thomas Maitland died in 1824, and a number of succeeding Commissioners adopted a more humane and pro-Greek approach. The last of these British Commissioners was Sir Henry Storks, appointed in 1859. A visit to the Ionian Islands by Prime Minister William Gladstone convinced him of the great desire of the islanders to be united with the rest of Greece. This wish was soon to be granted: on 15 November 1863 a treaty was signed in London by the Great Powers, as a result of which Britain resigned from her position as Protector of the Island State. On 21 May 1864 an official ceremony took place in Corfu by which the Ionian Islands became part of Greece.

In later years, Corfu became actively involved in both World Wars. In the First World War, a substantial part of the Serbian army retreated to Corfu (1915–16), and in June 1917 Corfu was used as the stage from which to announce the establishment of a new nation — Yugoslavia.

In 1941, during the Second World War, Italy took control of Corfu and the Ionian Islands with the help of Germany. In 1944 Italy surrendered to the Allies, as a result of which the Germans turned on the occupying Italian forces and bombed Corfu Town. British and American forces also bombed the town in an attempt to drive out the Germans, and many beautiful and historic buildings were destroyed.

In the days since the war, the Ionian Islands have seen no further violence, fine buildings have been restored and, with the growth of the tourist trade during the past decades, Corfu and the islands have advanced greatly in prosperity.

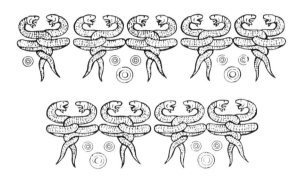

Activity 10: A Corfu time line
Design and construct an illustrated time line on the classroom wall to help the children appreciate that the complex history of Corfu can be divided into a number of distinct stages or eras. Add significant years, dates (e.g. key treaties), and headings for the key stages. The following stages are suggested:

  prehistoric period
  early history (734 BC–AD 300)
  Byzantine period
  period of the Crusaders
  Venetian period
  French period
  period of British protection
  from revolution to liberation
  period of two World Wars
  post-war peace and prosperity.

These various stages can then be pursued in as great or as little depth as desired, in terms of further research, written accounts and illustrations. Perhaps key sentences and an illustration of each could be written alongside the time line, and a class book could be made incorporating more detailed accounts. A number of suggestions for more specific activities now follows.

Activity 11: Archaeological evidence
A Discuss the evidence we have today for the existence of prehistoric settlements on Corfu. Exhibits in the Archaeological Museum in Corfu Town include fragments from the earliest New Stone Age (sixth millennium BC), including flint stones, pottery and tools from the Bronze Age.

B The Archeological Museum also contains many sculptures from the Temple of Artemis at Palaiopolis, the ancient capital of Corcyra. It is estimated that this temple was built between 590–580 BC. **Copymaster 3** (The Artemis Temple) shows the immense stone pediment from this temple and an enlarged Gorgon, which is its centrepiece. It is argued that this pediment is the most important monumental sculpture in the Greek Archaic style and references to it will frequently be found in books on the history of Greek art. Discuss with the class what this pediment shows. In its middle position is the Gorgon (enlarged in the copymaster), the work of a Corinthian sculptor, which measures 17 metres in width and over 3 metres in height. Measure out this distance in the playground to give the class an idea of its immense size. The monstrous Gorgon is depicted with wings and writhing snakes coiled around her. To the right and left of her are the children Pegasus and Chrysaoras. On either side of these are two lionpanthers, imaginary animals with the head of a lion and the body of a panther. The copymaster can, of course, be coloured and the drawing enlarged to make a heading for a wall display on Greek art or on the history of Corfu (link to art activities).

Activity 12: How did Corcyra (or *Kerkyra*) get its name?
A Tell the story of the nymph Kerkyra, whose name was given to the island. In the Greek legend, Kerkyra or Korkira was the daughter of the river Asopos. She was abducted by the sea god Poseidon, and from their union came Phaeacas, the progenitor of the Phaeacian race who later came to inhabit the island.

B If the children are old enough to appreciate the stories, tell them more about Homer's two epics the *Iliad* and the *Odyssey*, as well as other tales from Greek myth and legend. A number of good translations are available from which the stories can be read or told, and many of the heroes, adventures and monsters contained within their pages will capture the imagination of the children. This, in turn, could lead to much colourful artwork and creative writing.

It is believed that Homer's Scheria is today's Corfu. Refer to the late Bronze Age culture described by Homer in the *Odyssey*, in the section involving Nausicaa and her father, King Alcinous. Consult other sources to find pictures of scenes from Greek mythology, such as Odysseus escaping from the Cyclops, or one of the rare artistic depictions of Homer's *Odyssey*, such as the Sirens tempting Odysseus and his men (480 BC).

Odysseus escaping from the Cyclops

Odysseus and his crew were tempted by the songs of the Sirens

Activity 13: The influence of Europe on the history of Corfu

A As the Greeks began to turn away from Asia and towards Europe, a number of significant characters influenced the development of Corfu. Make an illustrated book of key personalities in the history of Corfu, describing their involvement and influence. Your 'roll of honour' will no doubt include the following:

- Robert Guiscard
- Napoleon Bonaparte
- Count John Capodistrias
- Benito Mussolini
- Sir Thomas Maitland
- William Gladstone

B Make a patchwork display or wall hanging in collage or needlecraft, entitled 'The Ten Ages of Corfu'. Divide children into groups, with each group creating one of the ten ages:

- Prehistoric Corfu
- Early history
- Byzantine period
- The Crusaders
- Venetian period
- French period
- British protection
- Revolution to liberation
- Two world wars
- Modern era

Activity 14: Corfu Town

A Find pictures of historic Corfu Town and talk to the children about them.

Background information
Despite the bombing in wartime, the town has retained its charm and relics of many cultures. There is no street planning, and many of the old, cobbled pathways are accessible to pedestrians only. Tall mansions with flower-filled balconies stand alongside English, Georgian-style buildings, Byzantine churches and Venetian steps and monuments. There are numerous green parks and squares. The most famous square is the Spianada which stands in front of the Old Fortress. Monuments in the square are a permanent reminder of events and personalities from the island's history, such as the monument to Thomas Maitland and the bust of Greece's first governor, Ioannis Capodistrias.

The Venetian fortresses are the town's main medieval monuments. Originally the town started to grow in the region of the Old Fortress, where it thrived in the twelfth and thirteenth centuries. When the Venetians conquered the island in the fourteenth century, the town expanded beyond the fortress walls. Later it required new fortifications and another fortress was built between 1572 and 1588. The Old Fortress stands on an islet, around 100 metres from Spianada. It is surrounded by a channel known as Contra Fossa, probably made either by the Byzantines or the Venetians, and it is joined to the town by a long concrete bridge. Today the channel is used for the berthing of vessels. The New Fortress built by the Venetians was called the San Marino Fortress and stands near to the old harbour. The English made improvements to this and completed its fortifications.

B Make a large wall frieze of the Old Fortress.

Legend tells that the Old Fortress had a passageway below the sea which led to Ptychia (Vido), the islet opposite

Activity 15: Desire for freedom
Discuss why the Corfiots were so determined over the years to gain their freedom from other nations and to become part of Greece. Let the children suggest reasons for this strength of feeling. Set against these reasons the beneficial aspects of rule by other nations, for example, the buildings provided by the British, the cultural aspects which are a legacy from the Italians, and so on. End this activity by asking children to write imaginative accounts of Corfiot feelings and celebrations on 21 May 1864. Illustrate these with drawings of the Greek flag flying over buildings in Corfu town.

The New Fortress

ENGLISH

Activity 16: How many names does Corfu have?
Head up a wall display about Corfu with alternative words for its name.

Background information
This topic has already referred to Corfu, the Greek *Kerkyra* (or *Kerkira*) and the more historic Corcyra. In the *Odyssey*, Homer calls it the 'rich island of the Phaeacians'. Other ancient names include *Makris*, because of its oblong shape; *Drepanon* or *Drepani*, because of its resemblance to the shape of a sickle; and *Sheria*, because the goddess Demeter asked Poseidon to stop (*shein*) or check the alluvium flow of the river across from Corfu on the mainland, so that the mainland would not eventually join with the island. During the Byzantine era, the name *Korifa* prevailed, deriving from the twin-peaked acropolis which stood in front of the site where Corfu Town stands today. The Bishop of Paramithia derived the word *Korifa* from the name of a church dedicated to the *Korifei* (or leading) apostles, Peter and Paul. The church then stood on the acropolis, and so Corfu is a corruption of the word *Korifo*, and its different grammatical changes in Greek (*Korifa, Korifous, Korfous*). The present Greek name *Kerkira* derives from the old myth about the nymph Kerkira, as previously mentioned (page 7).

Corfu

Activity 17: Become a Greek speaker
Teach the class some words of Greek. The following basic words will serve as an introduction to the language. Note that these are written in English letters and are pronounced as they are spelled. To pursue this activity in greater depth, one could of course teach the Greek alphabet.

English	**Greek**
Good morning	*Kalimera*
Good evening	*Kalispera*
Hello	*Yasou*
Goodbye	*Yasou*
Please	*Parakalo*
Thank you	*Efkaristo*
Today	*Simera*
Tomorrow	*Avrio*
Yesterday	*Efthes*
Yes	*Nai*
No	*Ochi*
My name is ...	*Onamozome* ...
One	*Ena*
Two	*Thio*
Three	*Tria*
Four	*Tessera*
Five	*Pende*
Six	*Exsi*
Seven	*Efta*
Eight	*Octo*
Nine	*Enya*
Ten	*Theka*

Activity 18: The literary heritage of Corfu
Introduce the class to the names and perhaps some of the works of famous writers who have had connections with Corfu. In particular, children may appreciate the works of Gerald Durrell, the author of animal stories, whose family spent extended periods of time on Corfu, and Edward Lear, mid-nineteenth-century author of humorous limericks and the children's classic, *The Book of Nonsense*. Note that Gerald Durrell's brother Lawrence wrote a travel book about the island, *Prospero's Cell*.

Literary minds which came from the island in ancient times include:

- Philiskes, tragic poet of the Alexandrine period who wrote 42 tragedies and lived around 284–247 BC
- Agallis, a writer who lived during the second century BC and became famous for notes on the Homer text
- Dracon, an author who lived in the time of the Emperor Augustus and wrote a work entitled *On Stones*
- Eumachos, an author and physician who wrote on the subject of the healing qualities of plants and their roots.

Background information
During the four centuries of Venetian rule, literary and artistic life flourished on the island, and in the centuries which followed, academies and societies were established to concern themselves with literature and the arts. There is ample scope for further research in this subject with children in the upper years of Key Stage 2.

Activity 19: Tourism and Corfu
Organise a class debate, 'Tourism: Good or Bad?', on the impact of tourism on the island of Corfu. Those speaking for the industry should emphasise how vital it is to the economy of the island today.

Background information
During the last few decades, life in Corfu has been significantly affected by the overwhelming presence of tourism. Most Corfiots are concerned either directly or indirectly with the tens of thousands of visitors who come each summer. They may work in hotels, restaurants, *tavernas*, coffee shops, night clubs, bars, beaches, souvenir shops or Government departments dealing with tourism. Furthermore, the economic life of the island depends on supplying the tourist industry: the fruit of land and sea supply restaurants, whilst local crafts supply souvenir shops.

Those speaking against tourism will no doubt suggest that visitors from every corner of the world have imposed a cosmopolitan way of life upon the Corfiots. The question can be asked: should the British presence be accommodated by the provision of fish and chips and discos (as it is in many tourist towns of Corfu) at the expense of the island's natural heritage?

Activity 20: Where to go on Corfu
A Suggest that the children produce some creative writing about possible excursions on Corfu, as suggested by a travel agent. (This activity could well be linked with geography Activity 6 in planning a package holiday there.) The following scenarios provide scope for creative writing: issue these to the children or let them choose a scenario they would like to write an imaginative description or story about.

- Experience the charm of a seventeenth-century village ... wander along cobbled streets ... discover craft shops ... wine, dine and dance the night away ... see spectacular costumes and Greek dances ... join in Greek-style entertainment.
- Visit the Achilleion Palace and gardens of Empress Elizabeth ... see panoramic views of the north-west coast ... sample local wines ... visit Makrades village for ceramics and embroidery souvenirs.
- Cast away for Turtle Bay ... cruise in a traditional caique ... swim in crystal-clear waters ... eat a barbecue on the beach ... see beautiful bays.

B As an alternative or extension to the above activity, suggest that the children write their own descriptions of island highlights, which could be prepared for a travel agency or tourist representative trying to sell guided tours to visitors.

SCIENCE

Activity 21: Plant life in Corfu

A Investigate the plant and animal life of the Corfu (i.e. Mediterranean-type) climate.

Background information
The usual Mediterranean species of trees, bushes and vines grow readily in the wild, aided by heavy winter rainfall. These include acacia, oleander, myrtle and plane alongside species such as wisteria and Lombardy cypress that have been introduced to the island from elsewhere. There are many wild flowers, including rare varieties such as the Corfu snowdrop (*Galanthus corcyrensis*), orchids (*Ophyrs pauciflora* and *Separia linqua*), a gladioli (*Gladiolus byzantinus*) and a member of the mint family (*Ajuga orientalis*).

B If appropriate botanic guides are available at your local library, let the children research these species and prepare illustrated documentation on the trees and flowers of Corfu.

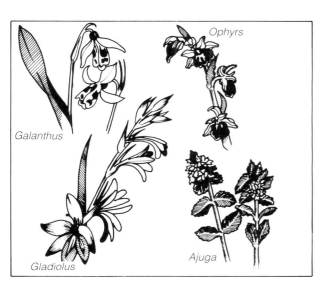

Some of the flowers found on Corfu

C Copymaster 4 (Edible plants of Corfu) introduces children to the range of cultivated plants grown on the island which thrive in a Mediterranean climate, and which are very important to the economy of the island. Let the children colour the drawings, add the correct name for each, and find out more about the cultivation of each plant and what happens to its harvest.

Background information
It is estimated that Corfu has around four million olive trees: the production of oil is an important industry. Grape vines are also plentiful — their fruit contributes to the production of both red and white wines. The kumquat tree was introduced from China and its tiny orange fruit is used to make preserve as well as a liqueur.

Activity 22: Animals, birds and insects of Corfu

A study of the animal, plant and insect life of the island could be another fascinating topic for research, if time allows.

Background information
A wide variety of Mediterranean birds and butterflies are found, and the island is noted for its many lizards, dragonflies and mosquitoes. There are few wild animals as such, but sheep, goats, pigs and chickens are kept in fairly primitive conditions.

Activity 23: Typical foods on Corfu

Discuss typical foods on the island and help the children to compile an appropriate menu for a *taverna*, with the guidance of the illustration below. Talk about how the menu reflects foods cultivated locally. The island is noted for its locally caught fish and particular specialities, which include *sofrito* meat (that is first fried and then baked with spices) and *pastitsada* (a braised spiced veal accompanied by a macaroni and tomato sauce). The Italian influence can be seen in the cuisine, as Corfiots use a lot of hot spices and tomato sauce in their cookery.

This activity could well be linked to the geography Activity 6 on planning a holiday in Corfu. Potential tourists could discuss sample menus of the food they would probably be eating.

Starters
Dolmades (vine leaves stuffed with rice and herbs)
Taramasalata (fish paste)
Tzatziki (yoghurt and garlic dip)
Keftedes (meat balls)
Olives
Feta cheese
Tyropitta (cheese pie)

Main course
Barbounia (red mullet)
Xifia (swordfish)
Garithes (prawns)
Octopathi (octopus)
Heli (eel)
Sinagrida (red snapper)
Tomatoes Yemista (stuffed tomatoes)
Moskari (Veal)
Pastitsada (braised, spiced veal)
Youvesti (roast lamb)
Sofrito (meat fried, then baked with spices)
Skotaki (liver)
Souvlaki (kebabs)
Koutopoulo (chicken)
Brisola (pork chop)
Stifado (stewed meat)

Dessert
Mandolato (a special nougat sweet in Corfu)
Baklava (honey and nut pastry)
Giaourti (yoghurt and honey)
Pagato (ice cream)
Peponi (melon)

Corfu

ART AND ARCHITECTURE

Activity 24: The architecture of Corfu
It is impossible to teach and learn about the history of Corfu without reference to the spectacular array of buildings and historical evidence, in the form of Greek art and artefacts, which can be found on the island. To draw attention to a small number of these represents merely the tip of the iceberg and, if time allows, do consult further reference material. Indeed, the history of art and architecture on Corfu would make an extremely worthwhile sub-topic in its own right for children in the upper years of Key Stage 2.

As a starting point, use **Copymaster 5** (Famous buildings of Corfu) which draws attention to five of the most famous buildings on the island, and can be used for a wide range of purposes. Discuss the age and architectural style of each building, its history, location and significance. Find out more about where, when, how and why each was built and what it is used for today.

Note that the names of these buildings have not been written on the copymaster, so that children can research their origins if you wish. Alternatively, names and locations could be provided in a jumbled form for children to match with the pictures.

Background information
The buildings depicted on the copymaster are:

1   Ionic rotunda in the middle of Spianada in Corfu Town, built during the nineteenth century in memory of the first High Commissioner, Sir Thomas Maitland.
2   The monastery of Vlakherna, off the tip of the Kanoni peninsula, also built during the nineteenth century and reached by a causeway.
3   The belfry of St Spyridon in Corfu Town. Spyridon was the patron saint of Corfu and his bones are kept in the church, which was built in 1596.
4   The Achilleion palace, overlooking Corfu Town, was built in 1890–1 and designed by Italian architect Cardilo for Elizabeth of Austria, as a retreat from the Hapsburg Court. It is a neo-classical and highly ornate building, set amidst huge gardens with sculptures and statues, including an 8-metre-high Achilles. Elizabeth was assassinated in Geneva in 1898, and the palace was purchased by Kaiser Wilhelm II. Today it houses a museum and a casino.
5   The Royal Palace at Corfu, also known as the palace of St George and St Michael, after the order established there by the British in 1818, and also the two names given to the two arches. It is an elaborate neo-classical building, erected by the British in 1819–23 to serve as the home of the Lord High Commissioner and the meeting place of the Ionian senate. In 1864 the building was presented to the King of Greece as a royal residence. It is now restored to its former state, and houses a museum with many works of art.

Activity 25: Icons and art in Corfu
A   If appropriate reference material is available, delve into the priceless collection of icons and works of art to be found in Corfu. Below is but one example, *The Virgin* (1494), located at the monastery of Paleocastritsa.

A fifteenth-century icon The Virgin

Note that the former Royal Palace in Corfu houses collections of mosaics from old Christian buildings around the island, Byzantine icons and even a large collection of Asian art and artefacts, mostly gathered in the twentieth century by Gregory Manos, a Greek diplomat who served in the orient.

B   Paint pictures or make a mural of a typical scene of Corfu architecture with a view out to sea, based on the following design.

Views like this are typical on the island

Corfu

C Use **Copymaster 6** (A rural house) to construct a typical Corfiot home. Cut out the copymaster, stick it on to card, pierce the slots, and fold along the dotted lines before starting to make the model.

D Paint a Corfu townscape as a wall mural to depict a typical street scene of today, with traditional town house architecture set in narrow streets.

MUSIC

Activity 26: Music and dance in Corfu

A If possible, obtain recordings of traditional Greek music on CD, record or cassette to enable the children to gain a flavour of the music of the islands. Talk about music and dances. If there is a Greek connection within the local community, perhaps a performance of traditional music and/or dancing could be staged in school.

Background information
Dances in Corfu have their origins in prehistoric times, especially the various festivities of the Phaeacians. Similar expressive dances continue almost unchanged, with lively steps, graceful movements and jolly rhythms. The most important traditional folk dances of Corfu are known by the names of *Gastouriatika*, *Kalamatianos*, *Tsakonikos* and *St George*. Men and women of all ages dance them in traditional costume.

B Let the children paint pictures of traditional Greek dancers and dances. Travel agency brochures may again be a useful source of reference material, though it must be born in mind that published pictures may relate to modern versions of folk dances arranged for night clubs, rather than the traditional dances described above.

C Discuss and (if possible) find pictures of instruments used to play Corfiot music. Traditionally, the folk dances are accompanied by three instruments: the accordion, the guitar and the violin. In nightclubs, dances are usually accompanied by the mandolin and the bouzouki.

The Ionian Islands

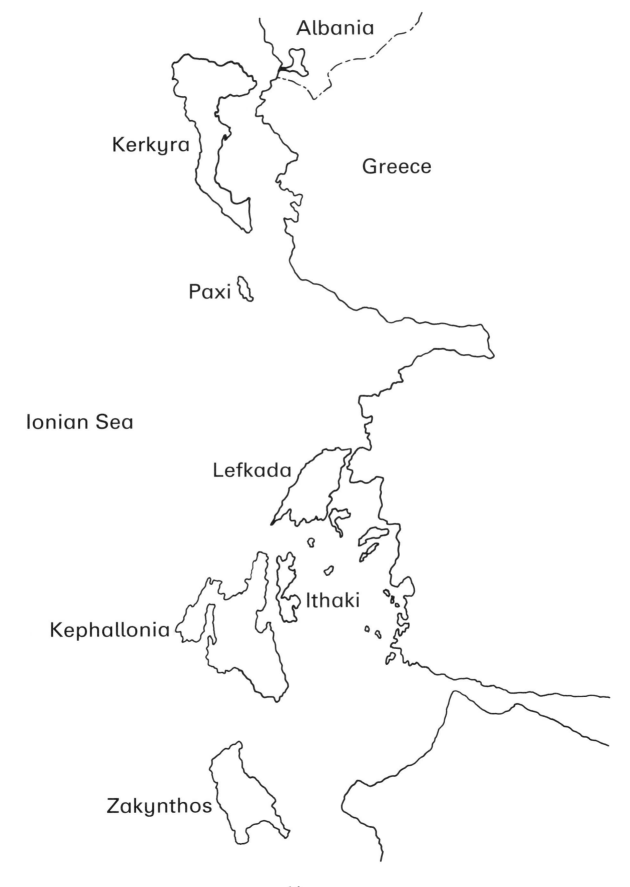

Kerkyra

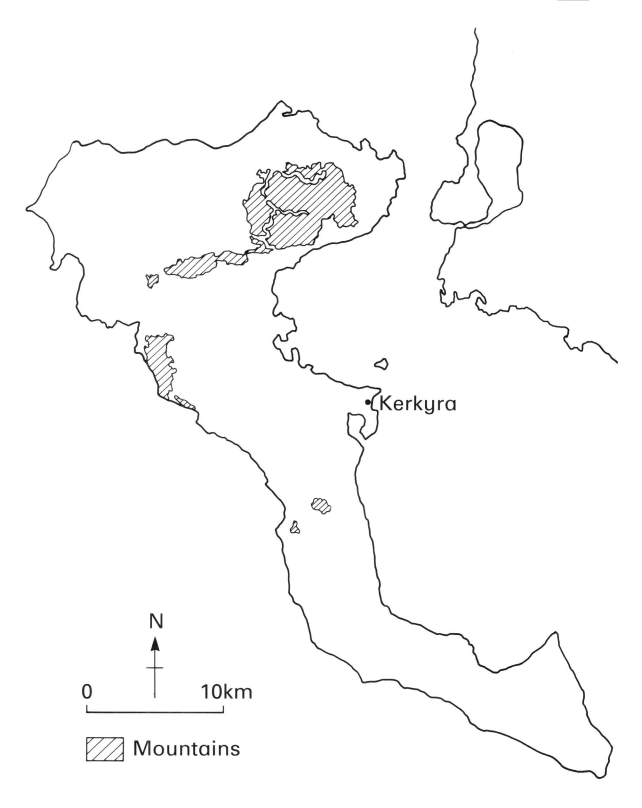

The Artemis Temple

The edible plants of Corfu

Can you add the correct label to the drawings?

Tomatoes   Almonds   Figs   Olives   Grapes   Kumquats

Corfu

Famous buildings of Corfu

1

2

3

4

5

A rural house

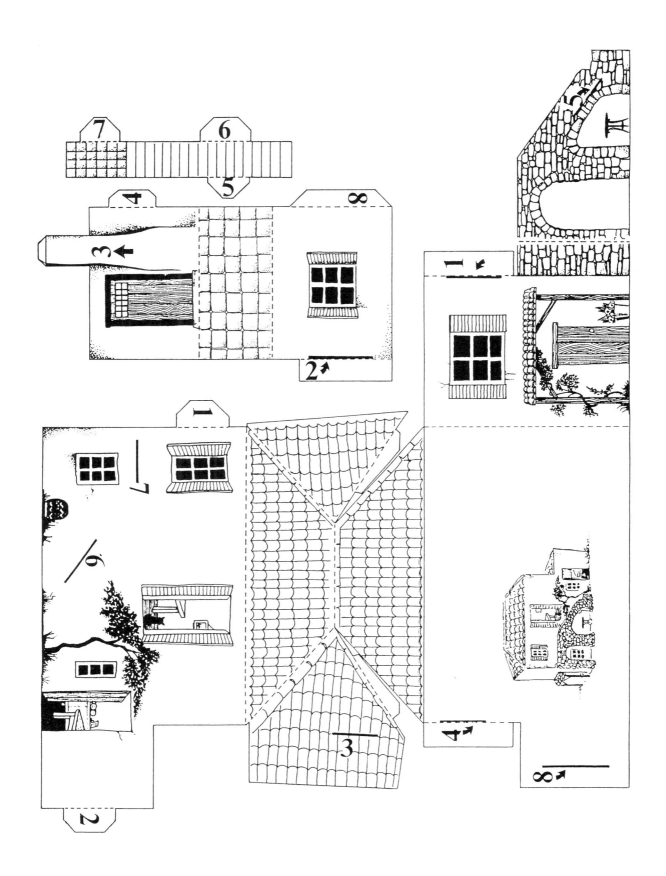

JAPAN

Geography
- Japan, the islands
- Japanese climate
- Land of mountains and forests
- Mount Fuji, volcanoes, earthquakes
- Leisure activities
- Bullet train: old and new contrasts
- Transport in Japan
- Tokyo: capital city
- Housing: traditional and modern
- Japanese foods — eating and cultivation
- Industries of the nation
- Japan's influence around the world

English
- Japanese names
- Stories, myths, legends
- *Haiku* poetry
- Japanese language
- Calligraphy

History
- Ancient Japan
- People of Japan
- Heiji War
- Feudal era — influence of Tokugawa Ieyasu
- People and events of recent Japanese history

PE
- *Judo*
- *Sumo* wrestling
- *Kendo*
- Overview of sports and martial arts

JAPAN cross-curricular links

RE
- Temple and shrine: the Buddhist and Shinto religions
- Impact of religions on everyday life
- Life of Kobo Daishi
- The tea ceremony

Art
- Nature of Japanese art
- Common art forms
- Scrolls of nature
- Well-known Japanese artists
- Genuine art exhibits
- Crafts of Japan
- Traditional music of Japan
- Films of Japan

Science and environmental education
- Wildlife of Japan
- Japanese industry
- *Bonsai* growing
- Fishing industry
- Oceans and conservation issues

INTRODUCTION

In total area, Japan is roughly the same size as the United Kingdom. It is comprised of four main islands, Hokkaido, Honshu, Shikoku and Kyushu, together with around 3000 smaller islands. Japan is situated in the western Pacific Ocean, near the coast of the Asian continent. More than half of the area of Japan is forested and much of the country is mountainous. Indeed, mountains run all the way down the length of the main islands, and there are many volcanoes, both dormant and active. Japan is also noted for the regularity of its earthquakes; around 1000 occur each year, though most of them are only minor tremors.

The country is not particularly well suited for intensive agriculture or commercial forestry because of its geographical and geological conditions. In fact, Japan is by far the world's leading importer of timber supplies. Rice is the main crop on the small amount of land that is intensely cultivated. Fishing is an important part of the economy: indeed, the Japanese fishing industry is the largest in the world, with major fisheries established along the length of the coastline. There are no mineral or energy deposits of significance, so the Japanese have to import almost all of their energy supplies.

The population of the country is extremely homogeneous. The main religions are Buddhism and Shinto, and there are numerous holy temples with their associated customs and festivals. Japan is an extremely crowded country where people live in small houses which take up little space. The total population of Japan is currently 123 460 000, of whom about 8 million live in the capital city of Tokyo.

Japan is the richest country in Asia; it is also one of the world's leading industrial and financial powers. Technological and manufacturing industries are very advanced, and the Japanese are particularly noted for their success in the car and electronics industries.

Japan is a country of great contrasts between old and new, tradition and development, eastern and western cultures, and between crowded cities and unspoilt mountain beauty.

GEOGRAPHY

Activity 1: Where is Japan?
Use **Copymaster 1** (Japan: the islands) in conjunction with a world map or globe to help children understand the location of Japan as a group of islands in the western Pacific Ocean, close to the mainland of the continent of Asia. Note the location of Tokyo, the capital city, and the names of the four main islands: Hokkaido, Honshu, Shikoku and Kyushu. The copymaster shows the location of the mountain range, extending all the way down the length of the main islands, and indicates the extensive forest land through the tree symbols.

Suggest that the children colour in the map, with the ocean in blue, the mountains in brown, and the forest symbols in green. This activity serves a two-fold purpose, helping even the youngest children to appreciate that Japan is dominated by mountain and forest, and promoting an understanding of the use of keys in mapwork. A formal key has not been included on the copymaster — let the children add this themselves in the space at the foot of the page. This sheet can, of course, be referred to throughout the topic, and other information added if and when this is considered appropriate.

Activity 2: How big is Japan?
Help the children to understand the size of Japan by explaining that it is very roughly the size of the United Kingdom. The islands extend over some 3000 kilometres from north to south. Expand this activity by considering differences in climate between the north and south of the country. There are more significant differences than one might expect in a country of this size, brought about by exposure to a range of air currents from the Pacific. The south of Japan is very much warmer, and the climate is such that tropical plants can grow while heavy snow falls regularly in the north. The rainy season is in the month of June, and typhoons often occur in September. Where children are able to cope with actual statistics and block graphs, the following information will provide a useful basis for drawing pictorial representations of temperature differences between north and south.

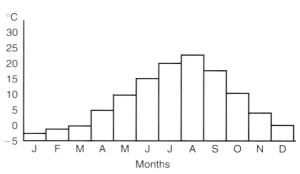

Sappora: on the island of Hokkaido (north)

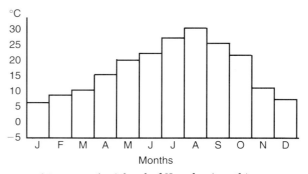

Kagoshima: on the island of Kyushu (south)

Activity 3: What is the country like?

A Discuss the significance of the mountains and forests of Japan; in particular, their presence means the inevitable crowding of lowland areas. The plains, where cities are located, are among some of the most densely populated regions of the world. Relate this to the fact that Japanese homes tend to be very small, so that they take up little space.

B Consult specialist books on the country for photographs of the Japanese forests and mountains. Discuss their great beauty, as well as their potential as suppliers of timber and electricity (with older children, you could develop this activity into an investigation into hydro-electric power as an energy source).

C Paint pictures of Mount Fuji, an old volcano which is the highest mountain in Japan, standing 3776 metres above sea level, south of Tokyo on the island of Honshu (see Copymaster 1). Pictures of this mountain are frequently included in tourist brochures on Japan. This activity could be extended to the production of a wall display, with paintings of Mount Fuji and accompanying writing on the subject of volcanoes, their origins and impact (cross reference with activities on volcanoes included in the topic on Hawaii, page 63).

Activity 4: Natural disasters

There is also the potential to explore the subject of earthquakes and their impact upon Japan. About 1000 earthquakes occur every year and, whilst most of them are mild tremors, earth movement of great significance does occur from time to time, causing damage to property and injury to human beings. The Japanese people need to be aware of this potential problem, and take appropriate precautions.

Perhaps the children could research or write imaginatively about earthquakes, and the precautions they think should be taken in case of such an event. Ideas and slogans could be collected together, illustrated and 'published', perhaps in the form of an 'Earthquake Code' and/or a series of posters of illustrated instructions.

The subject of earthquakes is dealt with more fully elsewhere — see activities in the topic on the San Francisco Bay Area, pages 42–5.

Activity 5: The mountains of Japan

Discuss how the mountains are put to good use by the Japanese people for leisure activities. Hiking in forests and on the hills attracts numerous visitors to quiet areas, whilst winter sports are extremely popular. As the mountains are so extensive, residents of all main cities can find snow and ice for sporting activities within relatively easy reach of home.

Activity 6: Japan — a country of contrasts

Copymaster 2 (The old and the new) is designed to help pupils appreciate some of the great contrasts of the country and link the above activities with thoughts of modern technology. The copymaster shows Mount Fuji and the Bullet Train, which passes this mountain on its journeys as one of the world's fastest train services. Suggest that the children colour the copymaster, having researched, if possible, accurate colours for the train, and add some writing about the 'Bullet'. Ask them to suggest why the train has this name, and to try to find out more about this train service.

Activity 7: Transport in Japan

A The above activity could well lead to a sub-topic on the various forms of transport in Japan. The Japanese are noted for their experimentation with new and improved modes of transport for both road and rail. The Japanese railway network carries more passengers than that of any other nation and, because of the nature of the terrain of the country, is ideal for long-distance transportation.

Consider, also, air transport. Tourist brochures are useful sources of photographs and information about JAL (Japan's international airline). Children could write to the airline and ask for information about craft in its fleet: Jumbo jets were introduced to the airline in 1970 and Concordes in 1976. Work could also be undertaken on investigation of flight times from London to Tokyo. With older children, actual times of flights could be investigated at the local travel agents, leading to discussion on world time zones.

The logo of Japanese airlines, JAL (reproduced by kind permission)

B Find out more about city life in Japan, notably in the capital city of Tokyo. Use **Copymaster 3** (Tokyo) as a starting point for discussion about this crowded, bustling city. The Japanese flag is included for the children to colour and serves two purposes: to familiarise them with the design of the flag, and also to provide the basis for a discussion on Japanese character. The people tend to be very nationalistic and care deeply about the image that their country presents to the rest of the world. The copymaster could be used as a basis for further discussion and writing about Tokyo as a place to live and work. The national flag has a symbol representing the sun. Its name is *Hi-no Maru*, meaning 'circle of the sun', since the Japanese believe their country to be 'the land of the sun'.

Background information

Tokyo has not always been the capital city of Japan. It was once a small fishing village called Edo. The capital was further west, once at Nara and then at Kyoto. In 1868 the capital officially transferred to Edo, and was renamed *Tokyo* meaning 'eastern capital'. A great deal of the city was destroyed in a major earthquake in 1923, and again during the Second World War.

As we approach the twenty-first century, Tokyo is one of the largest and most crowded cities in the world. It is very much a built environment, with numerous high-rise buildings and concrete flyovers. Little greenery exists, apart from that in a few city parks. Houses have little in the way of gardens and adjacent open space.

Activity 8: The city of Tokyo
Discuss with the children why Tokyo has little to see in the way of historic buildings and monuments. Children who do not live in an earthquake zone may well not appreciate their good fortune in avoiding the threat of natural disasters of this kind. If possible, find pictures of and discover more about some of the well-known landmarks of Tokyo today, such as the Imperial Palace, surrounded by moats in the heart of the city, the castle of the Tokugawa military rulers, and Tokyo Tower, a television pylon which stands some 332 metres high and is designed to withstand earth tremors and typhoons.

Activity 9: Tourist guide to Tokyo
Use further reference material and information derived from tourist brochures to write a class 'Tourist Guide to Tokyo'. Various groups and individuals could prepare entries on different aspects of the city worth visiting, perhaps including maps and advice on how to travel around the city and where to stay. Travel agents are an obvious source of information on some of the leading hotels of the city, whose pictures could be cut out and included in the guide book.

Activity 10: Houses in Japan
A Help the children to appreciate how housing in Japan includes aspects of typical and traditional styles, as well as adaptations brought about by modern, Western influences. The following information will be helpful, and could be written out as separate sentences (without headings) so that the children can work out which features are traditional and which the result of external influences. Children could then write descriptions of houses in both categories and paint pictures to accompany their descriptions in a display.

Background information
Traditional houses are very small with little space around them, and small or non-existant gardens. They may have a porch containing flowers or a display, sliding screens which change the size of the room when desired, and furnishings, including low tables and floor cushions. Wood is the main building material. Floors are made of earth or wood; roofs of thatch or tile.

Modern apartments are found in high-rise buildings; houses on developments with more space. Steel and concrete are used as building materials. The rooms are Western-style (e.g. kitchen, bathroom, etc.); living rooms and bedrooms are separate. All rooms have fixed walls and are furnished with higher tables, chairs and modern equipment, such as TV, refrigerator, hi-fi, and so on.

B Suggest that the children consider the above differences from the point of view of the Japanese people. Do they regard changes as being for the better? This activity could develop into a class debate on the values (or otherwise) of retaining aspects of tradition.

Activity 11: Japanese food
Find out more about what the Japanese like to eat, and how food is prepared and served. Once again, contrasts must be made between the traditional and modern innovations.

Background information
The traditional Japanese diet is based on rice and fish, for the obvious reason that these are locally available in abundance. Soups, fruit and vegetables are common components of traditional menus, alongside tea as a drink. These items are available from markets and small shops. The influence of Western life has introduced innovations into Japanese menus, notably meat, bread, milk, ice cream, coffee and beer. Along with new foods have come new methods of shopping at supermarkets and hypermarkets. Traditional Japanese methods of cooking include steaming, stir-frying and grilling, but again the Western influence has broadened the range of kitchen equipment and methods of food preparation.

Activity 12: A Japanese meal
Divide the children into groups to design, write out and, if possible, prepare a traditional Japanese dish or menu. This activity will, of course, be limited by the ingredients available, though most large supermarkets in the UK stock a sufficient range of goods to create an authentic Japanese meal. This activity could be used as the focus for a class 'Japanese Day' or festival, when children dress up in traditional costume and consider other aspects of Japanese life and culture, as suggested in later activities.

Background information
The Japanese do not usually serve separate courses at a meal. Food is served in individual bowls placed in the centre of the table and dishes are beautifully garnished and presented. Each person would normally have an individual rice bowl and a pair of chopsticks. An extensive range of international and oriental cookery books is available nowadays, from which other suitable recipes can be derived.

Japan

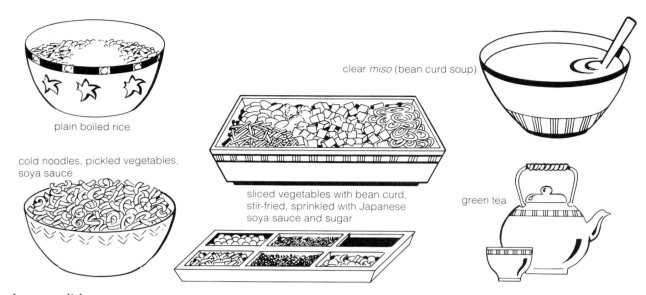

Japanese dishes

Activity 13: Raw fish and seaweed
Discuss the Japanese tradition of eating raw fish and seaweeds, two foods that will probably not have immediate appeal for the children! *Sashimi* is a well-known dish consisting of sliced raw fish, served with spicy sauces for dipping and finely chopped radish. Commonly eaten fish include squid, sea bream, bass and tunny fish. Another food related word with which the children may be familiar is *Tempura*. This is food coated in batter, deep fried and then dipped: common ingredients are prawns, oysters, sweet potatoes, peppers and aubergines.

Activity 14: Rice
If time allows, find out more about the cultivation of rice. Produce a frieze, perhaps with rice fields as a central illustration, and captions explaining the aspects of rice production as shown below.

Activity 15: Made in Japan
Ask the children to collect or paint pictures of as many things as they can find that are made in Japan. Catalogues from suppliers of electrical, photographic and electronic goods, and automobile showrooms are good places to start. Use this material to compile a 'Made in Japan' montage, which will form a focus for early-years understanding of the vast range of goods exported by the Japanese to Europe and other parts of the world. Older children can be helped to appreciate the dependence of Japan on overseas trade, its leading role as a producer of manufactured goods, and also its dependence on imported raw materials.

Activity 16: The influence of Japan around the world
A culmination of the entire project on Japan could be the production of a large display on 'Japan's Influence Around the World', with contributions from various

The plant
How it grows, life cycle

Diet
Place of rice in diet, cooking and serving methods

Paddy fields
Size, planting process

Who grows it?
Labour, when and who, mechanisation

Climate
Temperature and water requirements

Rice

groups and individuals on what they consider to be major influences which Japan has had on other nations. Examples could be represented in pictorial form with short captions: some ideas are given below as starting points for further investigation.

The purpose of this activity, apart from highlighting some aspects of Japanese culture, geography and history, is to help children appreciate that nations do have an impact beyond their own national boundaries. Sometimes this impact is positive (e.g. introducing ground-breaking new technology) and sometimes negative (e.g. the impact of invasion in times of war). Discuss the widely held view that Japan has had a greater impact on the world than many other nations.

RE

Activity 17: The major religions of Japan

Use **Copymaster 4** (Temple and shrine) as a basis for discussion and further research into the two major religions of Japan. The copymaster shows a Buddhist temple and the *torii* (meaning 'bird perch') which marks the entrance to a Shinto shrine. The copymaster also helps to introduce the vocabulary of Buddhism and Shinto.

Background information

Most Japanese people are Buddhists, and many Buddhists are also members of the Shinto religion. Individuals do not have to choose to belong to one religion or the other. Some of their beliefs and practices have merged over the years, whilst there are inevitable differences. Shinto is the most ancient of the religions, and is a form of worshipping nature. *Shinto* means the 'Way of the Gods'. These gods are not usually represented in human form, but rather by objects in shrines.

Buddhism was introduced in Japan from China in AD 552, and has had a marked influence upon Japanese culture through the centuries. Many native gods and beliefs were adopted from Shinto, and numerous Buddhist sects were founded. Two of the leading sects are Jado and Shinsu. Zen Buddhism, established in the twelfth century AD, is also popular, with its emphasis on self-discipline.

Other religions which are well-established in Japan include Confucianism, Taoism, Christianity, and a number of 'new' religions such as Tenrikyo and Sokka Gakkai.

Activity 18: Religion and everyday life in Japan

Using specialist books and tourist guides on Japan, find out more about the impact of the two main religions on everyday life (marriages, relationships, social conformity, routines, etc.) and on culture (art, architecture, ceremonies, etc.).

Activity 19: Temples and shrines
Suggest that the children use the drawings depicted in Copymaster 4 as a basis for designing their own paintings of temples and shrines, with an elaborate background. For example, they may paint a picture of worshippers travelling along the road to the shrine, showing one or more *torii*; or perhaps a replica of a Buddha, such as The Great Amida, a huge statue near Tokyo known as the 'Great Buddha'.

The Great Amida

Background information
Torii are usually made of wood, painted red. They are often found in extremely beautiful surroundings, perhaps even in the sea! On the occasion of a shrine festival, stalls selling food, drink (*sake*, a Japanese rice wine) and other goods are set up along the road side for the benefit of worshippers passing by on their way to the shrine.

Activity 20: A Japanese saint
Read more about Kobo Daishi, Japan's famous Buddhist saint.

Background information
Kobo Daishi (AD 774–835) founded a monastery on Mount Koya, which became the headquarters of the Buddhist sect of Shingon. The saint is famous in Japan for his deeds as a scholar, artist, poet and calligrapher. It is said that he invented the Japanese phonetic alphabet. He is also said to have performed many miracles, including causing the growth of a bamboo forest from his walking stick!

Activity 21: The Japanese tea ceremony
Find out about the long-established custom of the tea ceremony or *chanoyu*, which derives from the influence of Zen Buddhism. This is a splendid example of how serenity and simplicity permeates everyday life. The ceremony has rules for its conduct which have been in existence since the sixteenth century. The utensils used, the setting and the method of serving the tea are all characterised by grace and beauty. Perform a tea ceremony in the classroom with Japanese green tea.

HISTORY

Activity 22: The legacy of ancient Japan
Consult other resources to find out about ancient Japan, its people and legacy. Discuss sources of evidence that are available to modern scholars and which help us to understand the earliest civilisations. Mount a display on 'Ancient Japan', to which the children can contribute writing and artwork depicting relics of the past and sources of evidence.

Background information
Immigrants from the continent of Asia were the first people to arrive in Japan, though no one is quite sure of the date of their arrival. Several cultures have been traced from around 8000 BC: the Jomon culture is believed to have been the earliest of these, leaving behind elegantly coiled earthenware pots amongst many other artefacts. These early people lived under the ground and were nomadic, depending in the main on shellfish and nuts for food.

Legend tells us that the Japanese empire was founded in 660 BC by Jimmu Tenno, a descendant of the god and goddess who originally created Japan. Various immigrants from China arrived around 350 BC, and they were the first rice cultivators of the nation. They brought bronze, stone and iron, as well as a variety of pottery objects.

A clan which claims to have descended from Jimmu established itself as the imperial family of Japan in the fifth century AD (a lineage which survives to this day), although by the ninth century the power of the imperial family had declined and Japan was ruled by groups who governed in the emperor's name.

Between the tenth and the sixteenth centuries, the land suffered an extensive feudal period, with life being predominantly characterised by war and tension. Peace under numerous military rulers, who virtually cut off all contact with the wider world, followed for another two and a half centuries.

Japan's so-called period of 'modern history' began in 1854 when her ports reopened and international trading links were established.

Activity 23: Mongolian or Ainu?
A Paint pictures of the two main racial types to be found in Japan today, and let the children describe their features and, if possible, their origins.

People of Japan

Background information
The Mongolian type have Mongoloid features, high cheekbones, flat features and almond-shaped eyes. Their hair is black, and the skin a brownish colour.

The Ainu type have lots of facial and bodily hair. They have a whiter skin and a more Caucasian appearance in general. There are very few Ainu people left today.

B With older children, read more about the early civil war period of Japanese history and related battles. Suggest that they write about or depict in art form one or more notable events. The Heiji War (1159–60), for example, marked the end of rule by the Fujiwara family and the seizing of power by the Taira family. This was one of many military revolutions of the time.

C Investigate life in the feudal era, and in particular the life of Tokugawa Leyasu, a strong military ruler or *shogun*, who gave his name to a lengthy and notable period of Japanese history, the 'Tokugawa era'.

Background information
Tokugawa was responsible for bringing relative peace to the nation after the civil war period. He defeated his enemies and became *shogun* in 1603. In time, he abdicated, allowing his son Hidetoda to govern, but the real power remained with Tokugawa. He formed a system of administration, military rule and strict social ordering that lasted for two and a half centuries. The most powerful people in society were *daimyo* or territorial lords, who maintained private armies. All lords had to pay homage to the *shogun* and attend his headquarters for months at a time. It must have been a spectacular sight to see a *daimyo* procession making its way to Edo (the old name of Tokyo) to pay homage to the *shogun*. Wives and families of the *daimyo* were required to stay permanently in Edo: perhaps the children would care to speculate as to whether the *shogun*'s hospitality towards these guests was entirely charitable!

Tokugawa Japan had four rigid classes of society. These were (in descending order) *samurai* (warriors), peasants (producers), artisans (craftsmen) and merchants. The *samurai* were by far the most significant citizens in terms of privilege in society. This system of class derived from Confucianism, the Chinese philosophy which had great influence on Japanese culture. An interesting anomaly in this system is that, whilst the peasants were technically ranked second to the samurai, they were usually treated as though they were the lowest in rank. Merchants gradually acquired rather more power, especially towards the end of the Tokugawa era.

The Tokugawa period as a whole is noted for the isolation of Japan from the outside world. Ports were closed and foreigners were required to leave the country, though by 1638 Japanese citizens were not allowed to do so. The only visitors allowed in were Chinese and Dutch traders, who were required to stay in one port, Nagasaki in the south.

D Use **Copymaster 5** (Tokugawa Japan) to help pupils understand and appreciate some aspects of this period in Japanese history. The sheet depicts Tokugawa Leyasu, a small yet colossally powerful figure, together with pictures of the four classes of society. Suggest that pupils colour this sheet and write about each of the people shown.

E Organise a discussion on the effects of the isolation imposed by Tokugawa. Ask the children to suggest what would happen if the UK was similarly cut off from the world today. The effect of this in the Tokugawa era was to perpetuate the very rigid social structure, which continued unchanged for hundreds of years in relative peace. Go on to explain how the Tokugawa rule eventually ended; perhaps the children could guess who came to power.

Background information
In 1866 the Tokugawa family was overthrown by a group of *samurai* leaders from Satsuma and Choshu. This revolution by the *samurai* and the period following it is known as the Meiji restoration, named after the reigning emperor. In 1869 feudal domains were abolished, marking the start of Japan's modernisation. The four-class system in society was abandoned in 1871 and authority was returned to the emperor. Modernisation involved the development of industry, communication, education and military endeavours along the lines of Western models, so that the outside world regained great significance. Systems were designed and introduced which gained the approval of Western powers. In 1889, a new constitution was proclaimed which declared the absolute sovereignty of the emperor. By the time of the death of Meiji in 1912, Japan was well on the way to becoming a world power with a growing empire (including Korea, annexed in 1910).

Activity 24: The recent history of Japan
Investigate more recent history by focusing on stories associated with specific notable events and people. Perhaps the class could be divided into groups, with each researching and writing about one particular topic. Suitable items could include Emperor Hirohito, the 1923 earthquake which destroyed most of Tokyo, the Japanese attack on Pearl Harbour in 1941, and the atomic bombing of Hiroshima and Nagasaki in 1945.

SCIENCE AND ENVIRONMENTAL EDUCATION

Activity 25: The wildlife of Japan
Discover as much as possible about the wildlife of Japan. As a land of mountains and forest, surrounded by ocean, it is rich in bird and animal life. Suggestions could be given of particular species to investigate, as detailed below. Perhaps the children could draw or embroider pictures of species they have investigated, which could then be assembled as a class patchwork frieze or wall hanging. If done as a frieze, this could be surrounded by a painted backcloth of mountain, forest and ocean scenery.

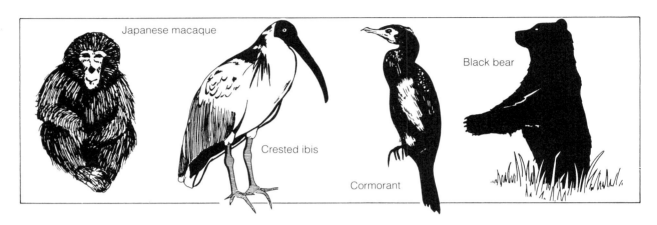

Japanese wildlife

Activity 26: Japanese industry
Design and construct a 'Japanese Industry' map. First, the children will need to find out about the major industries of Japan today (which could be linked to geography activities) and then design symbols to represent them. Younger children could simply attach painted symbols to a wall map of Japan to reinforce the link between industries and the nation; older pupils could locate the sites of major industries on the map, as precisely as possible. One benefit of this activity is practice in the design and use of symbols and keys for map interpretation. Pupils will no doubt enjoy the challenge of making up their own symbols, but help with ideas may be needed: some examples are shown below, which could be adapted into simpler symbols:

Activity 27: *Bonsai* trees
Investigate the Japanese art form of *Bonsai* (miniature tree growing). If possible, obtain a specimen and maintain it in the classroom, though it should be noted that these are usually very expensive. Find out which native tree species of Japan are suitable for growing in miniature, and more about how they are pruned and cared for (link with art activities).

Activity 28: The fishing industry
A Japan's fishing industry is the largest in the world. Find out more about this, in terms of types and quantities of fish caught, methods and markets. Help the children to appreciate that the industry is suffering from two serious problems: overfishing of many commercial species and increasing levels of pollution in Japanese coastal waters, which have reduced the number of fish available. Organise a class debate on the fishing industry, 'To Fish or not to Fish', leading to discussion of important matters such as fishing rights, the dangers of overfishing and pollution, and the need to conserve ocean life and halt marine degradation.

B Introduce children to the controversy over whaling and drift net fishing. Again, a debate is a successful way of helping them to appreciate various people's points of view, or a role-play activity could be organised in which various parties involved in the controversy are represented.

Background information
Japan leads the world in whaling and in the use of drift net fishing. This is a technique that has been described as 'strip mining of oceans', in that it indiscriminately kills large numbers of fish and sea mammals other than those which are the prime targets of the fishing fleets. Appeals to the Japanese to abandon this method of fishing have been made by various organisations around the world.

ENGLISH

Activity 29: About Japanese names

A Find out more about Japanese names. As with a number of other countries around the world, notably in Asia, a person's family name is put before the personal name, for example, Tokugawa Leyasu. Go around the class and let the children say their names 'Japanese style' — it will sound very odd to them to hear their names in reverse. Write out some names of Japanese people, derived from stories or reference books used in other activities on the project. See if any patterns emerge.

Background information
Many female personal names have the suffix *ko*, which is written as the Japanese character for 'child', for example, *Hanako* means 'flower child'. Common Japanese names derive from places in which family ancestors lived.

Activity 30: Stories from Japan

A Use traditional stories to help children learn about Japanese culture. There is a wealth of fairy tales, folk stories, myths and legends available, many of which contain ideas of magic and yet refer to important elements of the nation's cultural inheritance. Collect together as many stories as possible, and make a careful selection of those to be read out aloud and those which the children may read for themselves, perhaps with assistance.

Background information
The following collections are all suitable for reading, and are likely to be available through children's libraries:
Clarke, M. (1963) *Momotaro — First Folk Tales 3* Hart Davis
Crown, A. W. (1965) *Folk Tales Of The World — Japan* Arnold (two stories)
Fells, A. (1963) *A Tale To Tell* University of London Press (three short fairy tales)
Haviland, V. (1967) *Told In Japan* Bodley Head (five stories)
McAlpine, H. and McAlpine, W. (1960) *Japanese Tales And Legends* Oxford University Press (seven fairy stories and creation myths)
Power, R. and Watts, B. (1969) *Stories From Everywhere* Dobson ('Stories of the Magic Teakettle')
Scofield, E. (1970) *Hold Tight, Stick Tight* Ward Lock (six fairy tales)
Steinberg, E. (1966) *The Magic Millstones* Oxford University Press (nine stories)

Many of these stories contain fun and humour, as well as cruelty on occasions, as one might expect in fairy tales and legends. Animals, trees, birds and water have lives of their own, as do human beings. Some stories have no parallel in European fairy tales; inevitably their background, assumptions and values are different. For this reason, the best possible use should be made of illustrations in the books, helping children to appreciate visual images of Japanese culture and atmosphere.

B Develop one or more stories that the children enjoy through dramatisation and further imaginative drawing or painting. Organise a wall display depicting a favourite story, with creative illustrations surrounding the children's own written versions of the story.

Activity 31: *Haiku*
Read and compose Japanese poetry in the style of *haiku*, a short verse form. The verse contains 17 syllables.

Background information
Basho, a seventeenth-century poet and painter, is generally credited with the invention of *haiku*. Every school child in Japan today learns to write it. *Haiku* verse often has very distinctive Japanese themes, for example, insects, blossom, the seasons, waves, birds and rain.

Activity 32: Japanese ideographs
Study the Japanese ideographic language, at least at the level of considering the appearance of the script, which uses ideographs or pictures to express ideas, rather than symbols which stand for sounds. The script form was adopted from the Chinese language. If possible, show the children examples of ideographic script, and discuss the complexity of reading and writing it.

Background information
The relationship between the Japanese and Chinese languages is complex. The same ideograph may be translated in different ways by the two nations. Chinese characters could not be adapted in an ideal way to express Japanese ideas, and so when the language was adopted, the Japanese invented two 48-letter phonetic scripts to be used alongside the ideographs. Explain to the children that Japanese children have to learn around 3000 characters and two 48-letter alphabets in order to be able to read and write!

Japanese is usually written from top to bottom and then from right to left. Perhaps the children could try to write one of their stories on paper in this style, and see how many others can read and understand it afterwards.

Activity 33: Japanese calligraphy

A Use **Copymaster 6** (Calligraphy) to introduce this written art form. In Japan, it is frequently produced using a brush and black ink on rice paper. As rice paper is very absorbent, it is a skilled task to apply the correct pressure for each written stroke. Explain to the children that calligraphy is a common term used around the world today to describe the art of beautiful writing in various scripts. Translate the Japanese script on the copymaster. The characters mean 'I see beautiful flowers'. Suggest that the children copy this statement as accurately as possible in the space next to it, and perhaps illustrate their work appropriately.

B Older children may be able to research and learn a number of other characters from the language. If possible, obtain specialist calligraphy pens for the young scribes to use, reinforcing the skilled and artistic nature of the task. Alternatively, ink pens would give an authentic result, and are preferable to felt-tip pens for the purpose. (Many thanks to the Japan Centre Bookshop for their help with the copymaster.)

ART

Activity 34: Japanese art

A Try and help the children to appreciate that the term 'art' can be interpreted in a much wider way than is common in our own culture. To many children of primary age, art may well only represent a subject on the school timetable, usually involving paints and paper. To the Japanese, however, art is not separate from everyday life: art forms develop from simple everyday activities such as a tea ceremony, writing (calligraphy), *kendo* (fencing) and meditation. Discuss what *we* mean by the term 'art' and how, to Japanese people, the meaning of the term is so closely linked to other aspects of life. With older children, extend this activity by looking at a range of Japanese art forms (in books, museums, posters, etc.) and tease out common themes, including natural phenomena and personal circumstances (emotions, feelings, etc.).

B Discuss the distinctive forms of Japanese art, again with the help of secondary resources. These include scroll paintings, sculpture, ceramics, sword making, wood-block printing, gardens, flower arranging, and lacquer work.

Activity 35: Japanese gardens

A Find out more about Japanese gardens, flower arranging and art forms involving flowers and plants. Let the children make their own paintings of, say, flowers, bonsai, blossom and other natural forms. Perhaps these could be done on material or stiff paper, and made into a typical scroll, to hang up as part of a wall display.

B If possible, visit some genuine Japanese art in your locality, perhaps in a museum, art gallery or botanic garden where a Japanese-style garden may be featured.

C Find out the names and works of some well-known Japanese artists. For example, the eighteenth-century Suzuki Harunobu was one of the first artists to produce coloured wood-block prints, a source of inspiration for nineteenth-century French impressionist painters, whilst Katshusika Hokusai (1760–1849) was one of the nation's great landscape artists who also used wood-block prints. One of his most famous works of art is entitled *The Great Wave* (see below).

The Great Wave *by Katshusika Hokusai (1760–1849)*

D Engage the children in some of the typical crafts of Japan, such as weaving, fabric dyeing and paper making. Authentic pictures can be made if traditional Japanese themes are used, notably forms deriving from nature. Hand-made paper (see specialist craft books for advice on how to do this) can be used for picture making, or the construction of fans.

Activity 36: The music of Japan

A Listen to some traditional and modern music from Japan, perhaps from recordings available at your local record library.

B Some LP recordings were issued in the UK on the EMI label by a Japanese pop group, the Sadistic Mika Band, in the mid-1970s. By now, they will no doubt be very hard to find, though it may be possible to trace these for use in the classroom. One LP in particular, *Black Ship*, contains tracks entitled 'Typhoon' and 'Sayonara', whilst the title track is an attractive instrumental piece which should appeal to many children. The catalogue number of this record is SHSP 4043 (published 1974, Toshiba EMI Ltd).

C Teachers may wish to allow children a more light-hearted Victorian view of Japan, in the form of Gilbert and Sullivan's comic opera, *The Mikado*. Some of the music makes for lively listening, particularly the overture, the Mikado's song and items such as 'Three Little Maids from School': a number of recorded versions of the work are available. A copy of the lyrics for the children to follow is useful in the early stages of listening. Snatches such as the following will provide the class with a challenging tongue-twister!

To sit in solemn silence in a dull, dark, dock,
In a pestilential prison with a life-long lock,
Awaiting the sensation of a short, sharp shock
From a cheap and chippy chopper on a big black block!
(From the trio 'I Am So Proud', Act 1)

Having told the story, and perhaps explained the lyrics, it may be possible to visit a performance (amateur or professional) of the production, or perhaps to view it on videotape.

Activity 37: Japanese films

As well as obtaining documentary or travelogue films about Japan for the children to see, it may be possible for older pupils to watch and enjoy Akira Kurosawa's film masterpiece, *The Seven Samurai*. Since the film is in monochrome and also with subtitles, it might well be most advantageous to show the film as a kind of serial, in 15- or 20-minute episodes, followed by discussion with the children to reinforce the effect of the film.

Background information
Kurosawa's 1954 film was used as the basis for the famous western, *The Magnificent Seven* (1960), starring Yul Brynner and Steve McQueen. The plot concerns a village whose inhabitants are constantly plagued by bandit raids. They eventually decide to hire mercenaries to protect them, and the fast-moving action portrays their ultimate victory over the bandits, despite being greatly outnumbered. Kurosawa's film is rather slower in pace, since it runs for over three hours, and may well require judicious editing for children. Teachers may also wish to make a judgment about some of the more violent action scenes, though excessive pruning here could reduce the impact of the story, leading to anti-climax.

PE

Activity 38: Japanese sports

A The children will no doubt enjoy finding out about sports and martial arts which have originated in Japanese culture and are now practised around the world. Perhaps one of the best-known of these is *judo*, currently an Olympic sport. If any of the children or their parents take part in *judo*, then this will be a great advantage: ask them to come along and talk about their sport. Perhaps someone from a local club can be persuaded to visit the school and arrange a demonstration.

Background information
Judo means 'the gentle or pliant way'. In practice, this means using an opponent's weight or movements to one's own advantage, rather than fighting or resisting them. *Judo* players are graded according to their ability, changing the colour of their belts when reaching the next stage of attainment. Perhaps the children can discover how many different colours there are, and which coloured belt shows that the wearer has reached the highest possible level of skill.

B Help the children to learn more about *sumo* wrestling, the oldest sport in Japan. The first national tournament in *sumo* was held as early as 728 AD, but the sport was engaged in considerably earlier than that. Discuss with the children the attributes needed by a good wrestler: the sport needs a combination of skill, physical power and showmanship. It might also be of interest for the children to discover how much the average *sumo* wrestler eats each week in order to maintain his physique and fitness.

Background information
The average weight of a *sumo* wrestler is about 20 stones (280 pounds), though some are considerably heavier than that: one notable *sumo* wrestler earned the nickname of 'The Dump Truck'!

A long and symbolic ritual is performed before a *sumo* wrestling bout begins, and the match is usually over in a very short time. To win the match, one wrestler must push his opponent out of the ring or bring him to the ground. Only one part of the body is allowed to touch the ground during the course of a

Japan

match — the soles of the feet. The skills involved in this sport are very complex, involving over 70 moves or *waza*.

Sumo has recently been featured on Channel 4 television, so it may be possible to video-record bouts for the children to see.

B A third sport worthy of discussion and research is *kendo*, or bamboo sword-fighting. Children will enjoy painting pictures of contestants in their oriental armour. Indeed, all of the sports mentioned offer ample scope for creative art and craft work.

Background information
The sport of *kendo* is based on the old sword-fighting techniques of the ancient *samurai* warriors. These warriors traditionally used bamboo sticks for practice sessions rather than their lethal swords. Today, the modern version *kendo* is taught in schools throughout Japan. Fighters wear protective armour, and set about scoring points by touching specific parts of the opponent's body with their *kendo* stick.

D Make a colourful wall display of Japanese sports and martial arts, with collage pictures of major events and accompanying writing describing the rules, preparation and atmosphere of each. The three sports described above will probably form the centrepiece for this, but other common sporting activities from Japan can be included too.

E If an Olympic Games has taken, or will be taking place close to the time of the project, take note of the medal tables and discuss with the class the sports in which Japanese athletes seem to excel.

Japan: the islands

Japan

The old and the new

Tokyo

Japan

Temple and shrine

Buddhism

Shinto

A *torii*

Tokugawa Japan

Tokugawa Ieyasu

Samurai | Peasants | Artisan | Merchants

Calligraphy

私は美しい花を見る。

SAN FRANCISCO BAY

Geography

- Location of Bay Area in California, USA
- Physical features of the Bay Area
- The Golden Gate Bridge
- Other bridges of the Bay
- Bay Area weather
- Earthquake zone
- Earthquake intensity
- Earthquake precautions and safety
- San Francisco: cosmopolitan city
- Buildings and city architecture
- A rich racial mix
- Landmarks of the city

Science

- Baylands: zones of the tidal mud-flats
- Mud-flats and salt-marshes
- Ecological succession
- Profile of salt-marsh plant community
- Factors affecting salt-marsh plant growth
- Food webs and energy flows in the Baylands
- Birds of the Baylands

RE

- Impact of the missions
- Missions – architecture, restoration, controversies

SAN FRANCISCO BAY cross-curricular links

Environmental education

- Bay Area pollution

History

- Wall-chart time line: history of a city
- Bay Area explorers
- The gold rush
- Journeys to gold country
- Well-known San Franciscans
- History of the cable cars
- Story of Alcatraz
- San Francisco on film

Art

- 'Fog in the Bay' pictures
- Architectural styles
- Skyline of the city
- Bayland life pictures

English

- San Francisco — lively, bustling city
- The fog creeps in …
- Write a recipe book
- Story of the 1906 earthquake
- Earthquake newspaper
- An uncertain future

San Francisco Bay

INTRODUCTION

This topic focuses on the San Francisco Bay Area of California in the United States of America, and on the city of San Francisco itself.

The San Francisco Bay is the State of California's largest and best known estuary, that of the Sacramento and San Joaquin river systems. Before flooding occurred, the north–south trending valley was already in existence on the landscape. This river basin now has the butterfly-shaped bay at its opening into the Pacific Ocean. The northern 'wing' or embayment of this shape is known as San Pablo Bay, and the southern 'wing' is the San Francisco Bay proper. The combined Sacramento and San Joaquin rivers flow into the Bay Area at Carquinez Strait, and at Suisun Bay behind it, the two great river systems converge and flow towards the Bay. The spectacular gap at the point where the Pacific Ocean pours into the Bay is called the Golden Gate, now spanned by the world-famous Golden Gate Bridge. Inside the Golden Gate, the Bay contains more than 1036 square kilometres (400 square miles) of water, so great an expanse that the area could well be regarded as an inland sea.

Towering over this area is the city of San Francisco itself, built on seven hills. Within the city limits, there are no fewer than 43 hills, the highest of which, known as Twin Peaks, has two summits more than 270 metres above sea level, providing extensive views over the city, Bay and ocean.

The city's origins can be traced to the eighteenth century when it was a Spanish outpost. After 1846 when the city transferred to the authority of the USA, it increased greatly in size.

Today the city and Bay Area of San Francisco are world famous for a great variety of reasons, including their landmarks (e.g. the Golden Gate Bridge, the prison of Alcatraz, the Transamerica Pyramid, City Hall and the Opera House); places of interest (e.g. Fisherman's Wharf, Golden Gate Park, Chinatown and other Bay Area communities); items of note such as street cable cars; an interesting history which includes the devastation of the city by a substantial earthquake in 1906; and a lively, cosmopolitan, modern environment.

GEOGRAPHY

Activity 1: Where is San Francisco?

A Introduce the topic by helping the class to appreciate the location of the San Francisco Bay in California, in the United States of America. Use **Copymaster 1** (The Bay Area, California, USA) for this purpose. Look at the copymaster alongside a world map or globe, so that children can begin to develop an appreciation of distance and global scale. Locate the UK on this world map, and discuss the fact that the Atlantic Ocean lies between our nation and the east coast of the USA, and that San Francisco lies on the far (west) side of the great land mass known as North America. Explain that North America is made up of the nations of Canada and the USA, and that California is one of the 50 states which make up this Union. Discuss the fact that it takes more or less the equivalent time to fly from east to west across the United States as it does to fly across the Atlantic Ocean from the UK to the nearest point in the USA. If children are old enough to appreciate distances, discuss this in real terms. San Francisco is almost 9650 kilometres (6000 miles) away from England.

Discuss the content of the upper map on the copymaster, pointing out its key features such as cities (New York, Los Angeles), states (California) and the landmark of the Rocky Mountains. Explain that the lower map is an enlarged version of the state of California, helping to locate the Bay in relation to the coast and other features. This map has basic labels of key towns (San Francisco, Los Angeles and the state capital, Sacramento) and the neighbouring states of Oregon, Nevada, Arizona and Baja California, the latter being in Mexico. Suggest that the children add to this,

perhaps by adding red shading to indicate the site of the City of San Francisco itself, showing the location of the central valley of California, the Sierra Nevada mountains, and adding an approximate scale to the map (San Francisco is 563 kilometres north-west of Los Angeles).

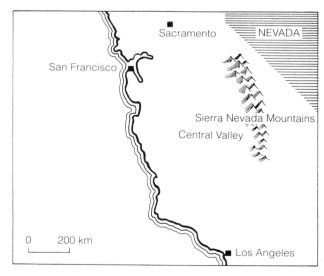

Site of the City of San Francisco in the Bay Area

B Continue the above activity and its focus on scale by examining in greater detail the geography of the Bay Area, as indicated in **Copymaster 2** (The San Francisco Bay Area). This sheet shows key physical features, for example, the Pacific Ocean, the two 'wings' of the Bay, the Golden Gate, the Sacramento and San Joaquin rivers. It also indicates the counties of the Bay Area. Explain that the State of California is divided up into administrative regions known as counties, in a similar way to our own country. Help the children to read the names of the counties surrounding the Bay: Sonoma, Marin, Napa, Solano, Contra Costa, Sacramento, Alameda, Santa Clara, San Mateo and San Joaquin. Discuss why these counties are not shown on the previous copymaster, thus reinforcing the importance of using a variety of map scales in order to show different landscape features. Locate the towns indicated on the copymaster: San Francisco, Oakland, Palo Alto, Sausalito, San Mateo, Berkeley, Daly City, Redwood City. Use this information to discuss the fact that whilst San Francisco is the key city of the area, there are a number of other significant communities (of which only some are shown) around the Bay. Suggest that the children colour the town dots in red, go over the county lines in brown, colour the water areas in blue and add a key to the map. Any other towns and features can of course be added as the topic progresses. The purpose of this copymaster is to provide an outline for individual use and elaboration.

Activity 2: The Golden Gate Bridge
Create a spectacular wall frieze to display work on your San Francisco project by painting a huge background picture of the Golden Gate Bridge to span the classroom wall. Discuss the history and other interesting facts about this bridge with reference to the following background material and the use of **Copymaster 3** (The Golden Gate Bridge). Children can colour this copymaster, and write accompanying facts about it. The background can be used for an elaboration of the drawing to include other aspects of the Bay and skyline of San Francisco, or as space for writing brief sentences or facts about the bridge.

Background information
The Golden Gate Bridge was constructed during the years 1933–7 and stands 61 metres above the Bay, spanning the Golden Gate. The plan and design for the steel suspension bridge originated from the engineer Joseph Baermann Strauss. Building it was no easy task: in the north, there were few problems, as the water's edge on that side of the gap was solid rock, but on the southern (San Francisco city) side, there was no rock on the shore and the pier had to be constructed on a shelf of rock below the level of the water, some distance into the channel. The current at that point was so strong that construction divers could only work between tides, for one hour at a time, four times a day, to prepare the foundations. Many accidents befell the construction task before foundations were laid, and a concrete wall had to be erected around the southern pier site, so that the builders could go about their task in still water. A number of workers were killed in later accidents as the bridge neared completion.

Today, the bridge carries six lanes of vehicles, and some 130 000 cars a day travel across it between the city of San Francisco and Marin County. The giant curved suspension cables measure approximately 1 metre (3 feet) in diameter. The bridge measures under 3 kilometres (2 miles) in length.

Activity 3: The bridges of San Francisco
[A] Compare and contrast the Golden Gate Bridge with the four long toll bridges (both suspension and cantilever types) that cross San Francisco Bay and the adjacent San Pablo Bay to the north. The first of these four bridges to be built was the Dumbarton Bridge, opened in 1927; the San Francisco–Oakland Bay Bridge was completed in 1956, as were the long 11.6 kilometre (7.2 mile) San Mateo Bridge, and the Richmond–San Rafael Bridge. Perhaps a large wall picture could be made showing the location of these bridges in the Bay, together with pictures of each.

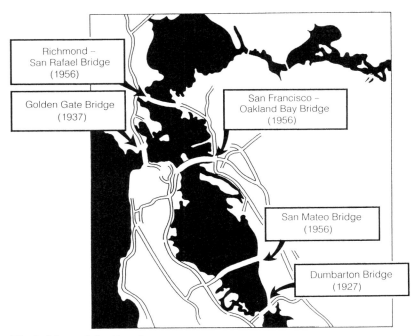

The bridges of the Bay Area

B Discuss the crucial importance of these bridges in the development of the city and Bay, and how they helped open up the whole area to industry and commerce, thus promoting prosperity.

Activity 4: The climate of San Francisco

Consider the weather of the San Francisco area: it is not as sunny as popular images of California might suggest. Temperature extremes are rare. Winters are usually mild, with January temperatures often around 10° Celsius (50° Fahrenheit), and summers never become very hot as they do in other parts of the state. The warmest month is often September, with a mean temperature of 17° Celsius (62° Fahrenheit). Rain is frequently heavy in the winter months, when torrential storms cause flooding and landslides on the hilly terrain, destroying trees and sometimes buildings. Summer months are noted for regular dense fogs which creep in from the Pacific Ocean. These are caused by cool air being drawn in from the ocean by hot air rising inland. Fog enters through the Golden Gate, and numerous pictures of the Bay show the bridge shrouded in fog (see art activities). Foghorns regularly sound to help ships in the Bay. Consult national newspapers which provide temperature statistics from major cities of the world. Collect statistics for San Francisco over a period of time and plot these on a graph. Compare the figures with temperatures for London or your home town.

Activity 5: Earthquakes

A Find out more about the nature and causes of earthquakes. San Francisco has been built on what is known as the San Andreas fault, a zone which is particularly susceptible to earthquakes.

Background information

During an earthquake, rocks in the earth move and sections of rock can be pushed upwards or may slip downwards. The name 'plates' has been given by geologists to the moving parts of the earth's crust. These plates fit together in a similar way to the pieces of a jigsaw puzzle. If they move closer together, they may form new mountain ranges; if they move apart, then volcanic rocks may emerge from beneath the earth's crust.

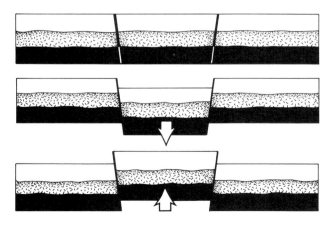

Sections of the earth may move up or slip down when an earthquake occurs

B Let the children design and construct models to demonstrate earth movement during an earthquake, as shown in the artwork below. This can be done by cutting rectangular cardboard boxes into three sections and painting their surfaces to show how movement is possible.

C Ask the children to write about what a geological plate is, and to describe what happens when these plates drift towards or away from each other.

D Help the children to understand how earthquakes can vary in severity. This will help them to appreciate that the 1906 earthquake which devastated San Francisco was big in the general scale of things.

Background information

The force or seismic power of an earthquake is measured by a seismograph, a sensitive instrument which measures the level of shock waves as they travel through the ground. These shock waves move outwards from the centre of the earthquake itself, which is known as the seismic focus. The epicentre of an earthquake is found at that point of the earth's crust which is immediately above the seismic focus: this is where most of the earthquake damage will occur. In 1935, the Richter Magnitude Scale was devised, by which the severity of earth tremors is measured. Scientists have been able to apply this scale to earthquakes that took place as far back in time as 1904 because of seismographic records. Earthquake magnitudes, according to the Richter scale, generally range from 3 to 8. The worst earthquakes ever recorded have reached only 8.8 or 8.9 on the scale. The San Francisco earthquake of 1906 had the equivalent reading of 8.3 on the scale — it was certainly a big one!

Activity 6: Earthquakes around the world

A During this project, scan newspapers for reports of earthquakes anywhere in the world. Read of their effects and consequences, and collect cuttings and pictures where possible. Discuss what it would be like to experience a major earthquake, and relate this to English activities and the story of the 1906 devastation (pages 44–5).

B Write factual accounts of how people in earthquake zones prepare for possible earth movements. Precautions in California include stringent construction regulations on buildings, adequate insurance, keeping breakables in locked cupboards, and knowing what to do in an emergency. Pupils will be interested to know that it is common practice to teach 'earthquake drill' to very young children in Bay Area nursery schools. Let the children practise what they would do in a real earthquake by crawling under a table or desk and holding their arms above their heads to protect them from flying objects.

C Design earthquake safety notices and post them on the classroom wall, perhaps alongside a display relating to the people and buildings of San Francisco. Your notices may be based on the following genuine example distributed at one university in the Bay Area.

EARTHQUAKE SAFETY NOTE

TO PROTECT YOURSELF IN THE EVENT OF AN EARTHQUAKE:

1. Remain calm — don't panic!!
2. If inside, stay inside — take cover under the furniture (desks, tables, workbenches).
3. Watch out for falling debris and tall furniture. Stay away from windows, mirrors and heavy objects.
4. DO NOT run out of your building — seek safety where you are!
5. If you are outdoors, try to get to an open area, away from buildings and power lines. If you are on a sidewalk near a tall building, step into a doorway to avoid falling debris.
6. Aftershocks may occur at any moment with nearly the same force as the original quake.

Activity 7: San Francisco — city of contrasts

A Using further reference material, help the children to appreciate the present day cosmopolitan image of the city of San Francisco, and its fascinating range of architectural styles and landmarks.

Discuss the many contrasts in buildings of the city, for example, well-preserved Victorian homes stand against a backcloth of modern skyscrapers. (Link with art activities and Copymaster 6.) Try and collect pictures of typical homes of the city as well as hotels and modern skyscrapers of the business and commercial district. Travel agency brochures should be a useful source of pictures. Cut out suitable townscapes or pictures of buildings and assemble them into a collage entitled 'A City of Contrasts'.

B Ask the children to suggest why San Francisco has such an interesting ethnic mix of people living there. In fact, the city has one of the richest racial mixes in the world. Almost half of the population were either born outside the USA or were the first generations of their families to be born there.

C Following on from the above discussion, make a list of tangible ways in which the multi-racial aspects of the city become immediately apparent to visitors. You could write these out on card, and use them as labels for your wall montage of the city and its people. Your list might include the following:

- people in a variety of international clothing styles
- shops selling ingredients for international foods
- foreign newspapers and journals on sale
- many languages overheard in the street
- whole city districts with people from other nations e.g. Chinatown
- banks of international significance.

Activity 8: San Francisco landmarks

A Use **Copymaster 4** (Portraits of San Francisco) as an introduction to further study of some of the well-known landmarks of the city. (Note that the drawings of the Golden Gate Bridge and Alcatraz can be linked to other activities, in geography and history respectively.) Suggest that the children research more of the background and interest of each of the features shown, write accounts of their significance and colour the drawings.

Background information

Fisherman's Wharf: Part of the 'Embarcadero' or port on the edge of the city, curving around the Bay. A well-known tourist attraction, where people gather to see fishermen and their boats, and to eat in one of the numerous seafood restaurants specialising in Pacific fish, and promoting local recipes and ingredients.

Chinatown: A district of San Francisco in which some 70 000 Chinese people live, forming the largest Chinese community outside Asia. The district, whose main street is called Grant Avenue, is characterised by Chinese restaurants, shops and businesses, as well as homes. Every year a traditional Chinese New Year parade is staged there.

City Skyline: The San Francisco skyline has many outstanding commercial buildings. Two of the best known, towering about the others, are the huge Bank of America building, and the pyramidal headquarters of the Transamerica Corporation.

Alcatraz: First a fort, then a federal prison (documented in history activities).

The Golden Gate Bridge: Dedicated in 1937, a 2.7 kilometre (1.7 mile) long bridge, built to span the entrance to San Francisco Bay.

B Suggest that the children research and design a second version of Copymaster 4, with pictures of other landmarks of the city. If the children do this individually or in groups, with freedom of choice of content, a wide range of buildings and features will be covered by the class as a whole. These can then be displayed to provide a colourful and comprehensive overview of leading landmarks of the city. If some suggestions are needed, consider the following:

- the conservatory, in Golden Gate Park
- the Opera House
- Coit Tower
- the Ferry Building at Embarcadero
- Mission Dolores
- Lombard Street (the world's 'bendiest' street)
- the Japanese tea gardens in Golden Gate Park
- the entrance gateway to Grant Avenue, Chinatown
- the Japanese Peace Pagoda
- the Palace of Fine Arts.

San Francisco Bay

ENGLISH

Activity 9: San Francisco — a cosmopolitan city
Suggest that the children write descriptive, creative accounts of the modern, colourful cosmopolitan image of the city of San Francisco today. One way of approaching this, after adequate discussion and looking at pictures of the city (in reference books and travel brochures) is to suggest that children pretend they are a street artist, sitting on the edge of a busy shopping area or outside one of the city's leading public buildings, and describe what they see. If you feel that the children need further help with this activity, provide suggestions for what they might see. Some examples are shown below:

- neon signs
- vibrant flower displays
- chic and elegant shoppers
- colourful buildings
- joggers, roller-skaters
- hurrying business people
- homeless people lying on the street
- beggars
- people of all ages and nationalities passing by, dressed in many different styles
- in the streets of San Francisco, 'almost anything goes'.

Activity 10: Feelings about fog
Compile a class list of words which describe a foggy atmosphere and related feelings (e.g. misty, grey, moist, damp, cloudy, smoggy, dense, swirling, shrouded, unreal, hidden, scary, creepy, ghostly, opaque, etc.). Suggest that the children use this as a basis for creative writing and composing poetry to describe the appearance of the Bay on a foggy day, or the creeping in of fog through the Golden Gate and the gradual obliteration of famous landmarks including the Golden Gate Bridge itself.

Activity 11: Californian cuisine
Ask the children to undertake research into well-known recipes associated with San Francisco and/or California. They could begin by looking at cookery books in their own homes: a wide range of international recipe books are published, and many general books have international sections within them. If some parents own books which are particularly relevant, perhaps they could be persuaded to loan them so that recipes can be discussed, written out and even cooked. If such items are loaned, emphasise the importance of taking good care of them, and ensure that a letter of thanks accompanies them when they are returned. Look out for San Francisco specialities such as sourdough bread and clam chowder. Perhaps a San Francisco recipe book could be researched and compiled.

Activity 12: The story of an earthquake
A Ask the children to write the story of the 1906 San Francisco earthquake in graphic, dramatic style. Provide them with the following historical information, so that their accounts can be based on fact, whilst including personal emotion and elements of imagination. These facts could be written out on sheets, or on slips of card for the children to discuss in pairs or groups before writing. Suggest that the pupils choose whether to write the story as if they were in their homes at the time or as an eyewitness account.

Background information
- Wednesday 18 April 1906: city wrecked by devastating earthquake, then engulfed by fire
- 5.13 a.m.: the earthquake begins 320 kilometres north of the city, travelling at a speed of 3 kilometres per second (over 11 200 kilometres per hour)
- streets moved like waves on the sea; buildings swayed like trees; church bells rang of their own accord; sleeping people were thrown from their beds
- tall buildings collapsed; debris flattened whole streets of houses and shops; people screamed and fled from their homes
- after 17 minutes, at least 50 fires had broken out around the city
- black smoke from fires caused darkness; the telephone system failed
- the fires were soon out of control: mansions and historic buildings were destroyed; homeless people wandered the streets amidst the rubble.

B Prepare a class newspaper on the 1906 earthquake. This could include some of the stories from the above activity, pictures, appropriate headlines, and representation of the facts in various ways, with maps, diagrams, statistics, and so on. Schools with access to desktop publishing should be able to produce eye-catching and effective results.

Background information
Assuming that this newspaper is designed to report the event and all its known consequences, the following facts will be of interest:

- over half the city population, some 250 000, were left homeless
- 28 000 buildings were destroyed
- the earthquake itself was responsible for some 20 per cent of the devastation — the rest was caused by fire
- 315 bodies were recovered from the rubble
- 352 bodies were never found
- the financial loss was estimated at $500 million
- massive aid from elsewhere in the USA and other parts of the world came in various forms: medicines, food, other supplies, and $9 million in cash.

C Organise discussions on various aspects of this story: for example, why the serious risk of fire is associated with earthquakes, why many bodies were never recovered (were they crushed, burnt, or shot by soldiers?), and the problems faced by insurance companies. As well as discussing the principle of

San Francisco Bay

EXTRA	**THE MARION CHRONICLE.**

News of the World Covered by Scripps-McRae Press Association and Other Special Service

VOL. 21. NO. 44.   MARION, INDIANA, WEDNESDAY, APRIL 18, 1906   PRICE 8 CENTS

TERRIBLE EARTH-QUAKE IN SAN FRAN-CISCO, MANY KILLED

Meagre Reports Have Been Received Over One Line of Telegraph---Indications are That 1,000 Buildings are Wrecked and 1,000 People are Killed.

insurance policies in general, explain to the class that many of the insurance companies involved in the earthquake of 1906 tried hard to avoid liabilities. Today it is often very difficult to buy earthquake insurance. Many large institutions do not carry insurance, as the premium paid over a number of years could well be more expensive than the cost of rebuilding in the event of disaster.

D Discuss the feelings that many citizens of San Francisco must have today about an uncertain future. Geologists are predicting that another very severe earthquake will happen in California in the near future, perhaps in the next 25 years. The epicentre will be somewhere along the San Andreas fault which stretches from north to south in the state.

E Ask children to suggest how they would behave if they lived in San Francisco, knowing that their lives could be affected in this way. Would they spend money on buying a valuable house? Would they wish to own precious breakables such as china, antiques and crystal? This activity could lead into a much broader and very worthwhile discussion with older children on the theme of risk-taking in our lives, risks that certain people are or are not prepared to take with their lifestyle, possessions, health, future, and so on.

By 1909, most of San Francisco had been rebuilt, to become a thriving city once again. Nevertheless, memories of the terror and devastation of the 1906 earthquake live on today in the hearts and minds of some of its citizens, and many more remember the earthquake of October 1989 that rocked the city once again.

San Francisco Bay

HISTORY

Activity 13: The history of San Francisco

A Tell the class something of the history of San Francisco, inevitably intertwined with the history of the state of California and of the USA. Construct a time line to indicate and perhaps illustrate key events in the history of the city. The following will form a basis for elaboration, depending on the depth of research you undertake from this and other secondary resources:

History of a city

- 1542 Cabrillo sails past the Bay
- 1595 Sebastian Germeno names Puerto de San Francisco
- 1776 Mexican settlers arrive in the Bay at a place named El Parage de Yerba Buena
- 1847 Yerba Buena renamed San Francisco, and the *California Star*, a newspaper, appears
- 1848 Gold discovered in the locality. California ceded to the USA
- 1849 Gold seekers pour into the city. City has a major fire
- 1870 Construction of Golden Gate Park commences. City population is 150 000
- 1873 First cable car service
- 1906 Major earthquake devastates the city
- 1927 International airport opens
- 1933–7 Golden Gate Bridge built
- 1934 Alcatraz converted from fort to prison
- 1963 Alcatraz closes
- 1964 Cable cars are declared a National Monument.

Background information

In 1542 the Portuguese explorer Juan Rodriguez Cabrillo sailed past the San Francisco Bay without being aware of the fact, as did Bartolomo Ferrelo of Portugal in the following year. In 1579 Francis Drake also missed the narrow Bay entrance, but landed 80 kilometres (50 miles) north of it in a place he named 'Nova Albion', territory which he claimed at that time for Elizabeth I of England. This inlet is now called Drake's Bay.

In 1595, the Spanish sea captain Sebastian Cermeno was shipwrecked close to the location of Drake's landing, and he named this strip of coastline *Puerto de San Francisco*, in honour of St Francis of Assisi.

In the 1770s, Spanish explorers eventually discovered the San Francisco Bay and started a settlement there. On 5 August 1775, the vessel *San Carlos* sailed into the bay and anchored. The following year its captain, Lieutenant de Ayala, returned with the first group of settlers, 244 people from Mexico. They called their settlement *El Parage de Yerba Buena*, meaning 'The Little Valley of the Good Herb', after a vine found in the area. It was not until 1847 that Yerba Buena was renamed San Francisco after the original name given to Cermeno's coastal strip further north.

Franciscan friars established a mission in the area, known as Mission Dolores, built with the chief aim of converting the local Indians to the Christian faith. By 1800, around 30 000 Indians had accepted the Catholic faith preached by the friars of San Francisco. At this time, four missions existed in the Bay Area, and to this day one district of the city is known as the Mission, while the Mission Dolores remains an active church.

In 1833 the mission lands of California were secularised by the Mexican government, which had gained independence from Spain in 1821. The Bay Area missions became parish churches for their surrounding communities, and they serve as a strong reminder of the Spanish influence that once dominated San Francisco.

In 1846 war broke out between Mexico and the USA. One of the causes of this was an offer by the USA to buy all the land of California for $25 million. On 9 July 1846, the USS *Portsmouth* sailed into the San Francisco Bay, meeting little opposition from the Mexicans. Captain John Montgomery took possession of California, and the United States flag was raised. The majority of Mexicans living in San Francisco at that time fled south, leaving a civilian population of about 450 people.

This situation was soon to change dramatically. In 1848 gold was discovered about 160 kilometres (100 miles) inland from the Bay, and as a result hundreds of prospectors flocked into the area: the gold rush had begun and the city of San Francisco grew apace. Many new streets of flimsy wooden buildings were rapidly constructed, soon to be devastated by the first of six serious outbreaks of fire that the city had to endure. San Francisco was constantly rebuilt and soon prospered as more gold deposits were found in the area. In 1859 silver deposits were discovered in the nearby Sierra Nevada.

By 1870 the city had a population of around 150 000, including thousands of Chinese, many of whom served as labourers in the construction of the Central Pacific and Union Pacific railroad lines (which met in Utah, thus completing the first transcontinental rail route).

With growing numbers of people and increasing prosperity came the creation of well-known buildings and landmarks: in 1870 construction of the world-famous Golden Gate Park began; in 1873 Andrew Hallidie began the first cable car service on Clay Street; in 1876 electric lighting was introduced in the city; the Ferry Building was completed in 1898; 1899 saw the opening of the San Francisco campus of California State University; and the Bank of America was established in the city in 1904.

One of the most dramatic and memorable events in the history of San Francisco was the major earthquake of 1906. This is documented elsewhere (see geography and English activities). The ensuing fire destroyed four-fifths of the city, and a major rebuilding programme took place during the three years that followed.

Since the 1906 earthquake, San Francisco has continued to grow and prosper as one of the world's leading cities. An international airport opened just south of the city in 1927, and the Golden Gate Bridge was constructed between 1933 and 1937. By the time America declared war on Japan following the attack on Pearl Harbour in 1941, San Francisco was the fourth busiest port in the whole of the USA.

Later years have seen the city develop into a thriving, cosmopolitan and, in many respects, controversial place. In the 1960s it was noted for 'Flower Power' and student protest focused on a range of issues including civil rights and the war in Vietnam. San Francisco has seen racial controversies, mass immigration, the hippie movement and an upsurge of interest in nonconformist values.

San Francisco must be regarded as one of the most fascinating cities in the world, in part brought out by its history. Hardly any of its present-day citizens were born there. Residents have come from near and far, creating a rich racial and cultural mix.

B Let the children hear some of the 1960s popular songs relating to San Francisco, for example, Scott McKenzie's 'San Francisco' recorded on CBS Records in 1967 at the height of Flower Power, 'Let's go to San Francisco' by the Flower Pot Men, and of course Tony Bennett's 'I Left My Heart in San Francisco'. Indeed, the lyrics of the latter song might repay further study as a poetic description of the city.

Activity 14: Early explorers in the Bay
Find out more about the motives and routes of the early explorers of the Bay Area: Cabrillo, Ferrelo, Drake and Cermeno. Plot their journeys on a world map, and write accounts of why the Portuguese and Spanish captains were sailing in the Pacific (i.e. seeking the North-west Passage).

Activity 15: The gold rush
A Pursue further investigation of the discovery of gold and the subsequent gold rush in California.

Background information
Gold was discovered in 1848 by a carpenter, James Marshall, at John Sutter's sawmill on the American River in the foothills of the Sierra Nevada mountain range. In 1849, the first gold rush steamer called *California* arrived from New York, and marked the beginning of a regular steamboat service between the American east and west. Thousands of gold-seekers poured into San Francisco. They were nicknamed '49ers: perhaps the children would like to discuss the origin of this nickname. They may also be interested to know that it is still associated with the city today, through the San Francisco American football team who have the same name. If possible, consult further books and suggest that the children paint pictures of the original '49ers panning for gold.

B Suggest that the children write imaginary stories telling of the long, hard journeys, hopes and expectations of people travelling from the east in search of gold. Some struggled across land but the majority travelled by sea, paying as much as $1000 each for the journey around Cape Horn.

Background information
The gold rush resulted in a massive expansion of the steamship industry. In the ten years from 1849–59, the Pacific Mail Steamship Company, owners of the *California*, built 29 vessels that carried 175 000 people to San Francisco. Many casualties occurred en route: between 1851 and 1853, 11 steamships sank on the voyage around Cape Horn and thousands of passengers died from disease, which was rife in the cramped, unhealthy conditions at sea. For those who survived, the six-month voyage must have seemed desperately long and uncomfortable, whilst food and water were scarce or virtually non-existent.

C Ask the children to imagine what conditions aboard ship must have been like on the voyage to California. Perhaps they can suggest how passengers may have occupied their time: one way was by singing. Write out and sing the words of one song which became well known: it is said to have been sung on the ship *Eliza* which set sail from Massachusetts in 1848:

> I came from Salem City
> With a washbowl on my knee,
> I'm going to California
> The gold dust for to see.
>
> It rained all night the day I left,
> The weather it was dry,
> The sun so hot I froze to death,
> Oh, brothers don't you cry.
>
> **Chorus**
> Oh! California,
> That's the land for me!
> I'm going to Sacramento
> With a washbowl on my knee.
> (Sung to the tune of 'Oh, Susannah!')

In its many variations, this song became the theme song of the gold-seeking '49ers. Why should anyone travel with a washbowl on their knee?

Activity 16: Famous names from the past
Find out more about the lives and activities of some of the individuals who made great fortunes in San Francisco during the days of the gold rush (unlike many thousands who did not!), and whose names became well known in the history of the city. These might include the following:

Background information
Peter Donahue arrived in 1849 and set up the Union Iron Works to manufacture pans and tools for gold miners. Ten years later, he employed 120 people and had machinery worth $150 000.

Levi Strauss, a Bavarian who had emigrated to New York, joined the gold seekers in 1850. He took cloth, needles and thread to the west and set up a clothing industry that was to mushroom into a colossal international enterprise. His products are found all over the world today — can the children recall the most famous of them?

Domingo Ghirardelli, an Italian, also arrived around 1850, having delivered chocolate in Guatemala. He sold chocolate to the miners and, as a result of great success, later branched out into the sales of coffee, mustard and spices. Ghirardelli's name can still be seen today on a building on the San Francisco waterfront.

Activity 17: 'To be where little cable cars Climb half-way to the stars ...'

A Paint a frieze of the famous street cable cars of San Francisco, and explore their origins and technology.

Background information
The first cable car service began in 1873, to replace horse-drawn trams. The system uses passenger cars drawn by steel cables that move in channels 46 centimetres below the level of the street. Since 1955 the cars have been protected under the City Charter, and in 1964 they were declared a National Historic Landmark, giving some indication of the great significance they hold. Today the cable cars are a great tourist attraction, as well as being functional in conveying passengers over some of the steepest hills in the city.

B Tell the story associated with the origin of these cable cars. It is said that Andrew Hallidie, the owner of a wire rope and cable company, witnessed an accident involving a horse-drawn tram. One of the horses pulling the tram stumbled, the tram's brakes failed, and the vehicle went crashing down the hill. Thus Hallidie decided to introduce a safer form of transport that did not endanger animals or people.

Activity 18: Alcatraz

A Find out more about Alcatraz, the famous island prison in the middle of the San Francisco Bay. Note that a drawing of this is included on Copymaster 4, described in Activity 8.

Background information
Alcatraz Island was originally a US army fort, and was converted into a federal prison in 1934. The prison was closed in 1963 to save costs, and the island is now a tourist attraction, made famous by films such as *Birdman of Alcatraz* and the more recent *Escape from Alcatraz*.

In the early 1970s, the site was illegally occupied by 800 American Indians who were demonstrating against White oppression, claiming that a treaty of 1868 allowed Indians to take possession of federal land that was unoccupied. Eventually the squatters were evicted by armed forces of the US government.

B Ask the children to suggest why Alcatraz Island was an ideal location for a prison. Suggest that they paint pictures or sketch the grim-looking buildings and

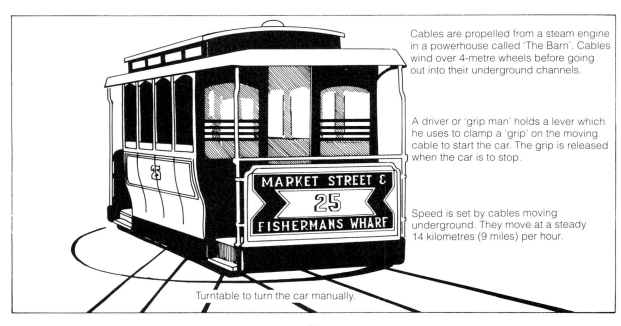

Cables are propelled from a steam engine in a powerhouse called 'The Barn'. Cables wind over 4-metre wheels before going out into their underground channels.

A driver or 'grip man' holds a lever which he uses to clamp a 'grip' on the moving cable to start the car. The grip is released when the car is to stop.

Speed is set by cables moving underground. They move at a steady 14 kilometres (9 miles) per hour.

Turntable to turn the car manually.

write their own imaginary stories entitled 'Escape from Alcatraz', which could have a modern-day or historical setting.

[C] Research and tell the children stories of some of the criminals who have been imprisoned in Alcatraz: they include the infamous Al Capone and Robert Stroud. Stroud spent over 60 years in prison for murder, devoting much of his time to becoming an expert ornithologist.

Activity 19: San Francisco on film
San Francisco has for many years been featured as the setting for numerous films, including the Clint Eastwood 'Dirty Harry' series, *Bullitt* with Steve McQueen (featuring an exciting car chase through the streets of San Francisco) and many other crime/detective films for TV and cinema. Towards the end of the topic, it may be possible to show extracts from some of these films which will show the city of San Francisco to good effect.

SCIENCE

Activity 20: The wildlife of the San Francisco Bay Area
Develop a substantial sub-topic on the ecology and natural habitats of the San Francisco Bay wetlands, investigating plant, bird, animal and insect life. The following background information is important for understanding the nature of the fascinating natural communities of the area, and could be made available to the class as reference material in an appropriate form.

Background information
Geologically, the San Francisco Bay is a classic example of a drowned river mouth. Before the estuary was drowned, the river's valley already existed in its north-south direction; thus, when subsidence of the land caused the area to be flooded, it created the butterfly shape of the Bay Area as we see it on maps today.

This estuary contains vast areas of tidal flatlands which are rich in wildlife, particularly birds and invertebrate creatures. There are two major types of waterlogged environment found in the region: mud-flats and salt-marshes. Often the two terms are used interchangeably, though there are differences between them. Marshes are higher than mud-flats and usually have much more vegetation which is adapted to living in an environment on the fringe of land and water. Small creeks of water run through the marshes, carrying the run-off and floodwater from both the tide and freshwater streams which flow in from the surrounding hills. Marshes are usually above the average level of high tide and their plants cannot tolerate permanently living in water. Mud-flats, on the other hand, occur between mean high and low tide levels, so their vegetation is of a more aquatic form. Deeper channels of the flats are permanently flooded. The eel-grass habitat (see Copymaster 5), for example, is usually under water, that is, below the level of mean low tide. Cordgrass and pickleweed, on the other hand, are intertidal plants. Cordgrass can tolerate up to 20 hours of continuous submergence in water.

The San Francisco Bay is gradually being filled in. Whilst this is in part artificial, due to reclamation by human intervention, it is also a natural process. Despite the fact that parts of the Bay shoreline have subsided due to the pumping out of underground water, thousands of tons of silt are constantly being dumped by streams and rivers entering the Bay. As the floor of the Bay is thus built up, certain parts of the land are raised above critical levels for the growth of certain plant species. Cordgrass, for example, becomes established and helps to stabilise new mud deposits. Through this process, mud-flats gradually change to marsh. It is estimated that even without human interference, it will not take long (in geological terms!) for much of the San Francisco Bay to become marsh, and then meadowland.

Activity 21: Life in the mud-flats
Use **Copymaster 5** (The San Francisco Bay) as the basis for discussing the various zones of the tidal mud-flats, examples of plant and invertebrate life found there, and the differing requirements of life forms. Suggest that the children study the copymaster drawing carefully, looking at the water levels and aspects which are permanent mud-flat 'land'. Explain that the two water levels represent high and low tides. Ask the children to colour the land and the two water levels in different shades, and perhaps add a key to the diagram. Discuss which plants and creatures are permanently in water, and which are between or above tide levels. Colour the life forms shown, and use further reference material to find out more about them. A sub-topic on salt-water invertebrate life could well be pursued, with details of classification, food chains and life cycles.

San Francisco Bay

Activity 22: Mud-flat to salt-marsh

A Explain the process of the natural infilling of the Baylands with deposits of mud and silt, and the role of plants such as cordgrass in stabilising new deposits. Link this to a discussion of the differences between the two forms of waterlogged environment, and introduce the key scientific concept of the succession from mud-flat to salt-marsh. Suggest that the children draw or paint pairs of annotated pictures of salt-marsh and mud-flat landscapes, depicting and explaining their differences.

B Make a class display of four pictures to explain the likely succession of areas of the Baylands from water to mud-flat to marsh to meadow environment. These could be large collage pictures designed for the classroom wall, based, perhaps, on children's own drawings and explanations of infilling and habitat change in their workbooks. Explain that the Bay is not likely to be infilled in its entirety, as it is the estuary of major river systems, though substantial areas of land could be established within it as a result of natural infilling.

C Extend the preceding discussion and activities on salt-marshes by drawing and annotating a large wall diagram to show a typical salt-marsh profile. The following artwork should form a basis for this.

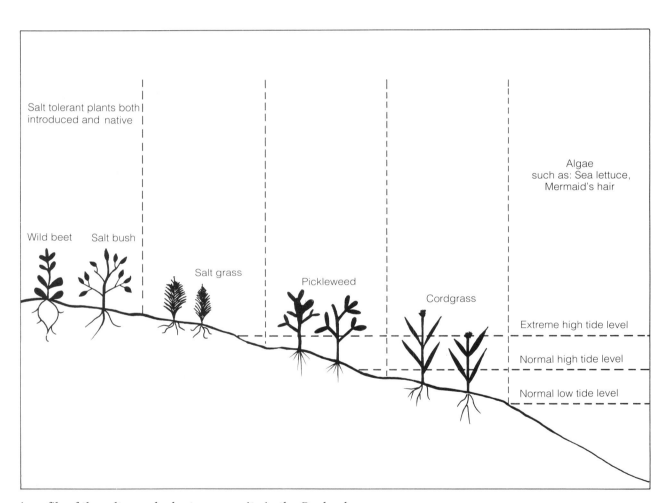

A profile of the salt-marsh plant community in the Baylands

D Consolidate these various activities on mud and marsh communities by helping the children to understand and appreciate major factors which limit the growth of certain plants, so that they are found in 'bands' or zones. A summary of the key factors in the previous diagram would be helpful. These factors are:

- the shape or slope of the land
- the amount of salt in the soil and water
- the temperature of the water
- the rise and fall of the water, i.e. the tides (caused by the pull of gravity from the moon and sun on the water of the Earth).

E If this sub-topic in science is being pursued in depth, then a large wall diagram could be built up to show food webs and energy flows in a salt-marsh, based on the content suggested in the artwork below. The background could be painted, and collage creatures and large printed labels attached. An explanation of some of the basic scientific concepts could be provided alongside, as in the artwork below. This food web and energy flow diagram shows part of the energy flow patterns and food chains in the salt-marshes of the San Francisco Bay. The arrows show the direction in which energy flows.

Foods (nutrients) are cycled in the direction of the arrows: algae, for example, is eaten by ducks, worms are eaten by birds.

Note that a wide range of scientific concepts are involved in this activity. It could well be linked to on-going science topics on energy, food chains, food/nutrients and life cycles. The activity could also lead to detailed investigation into the life and feeding habits of all of the forms of life indicated on the diagram.

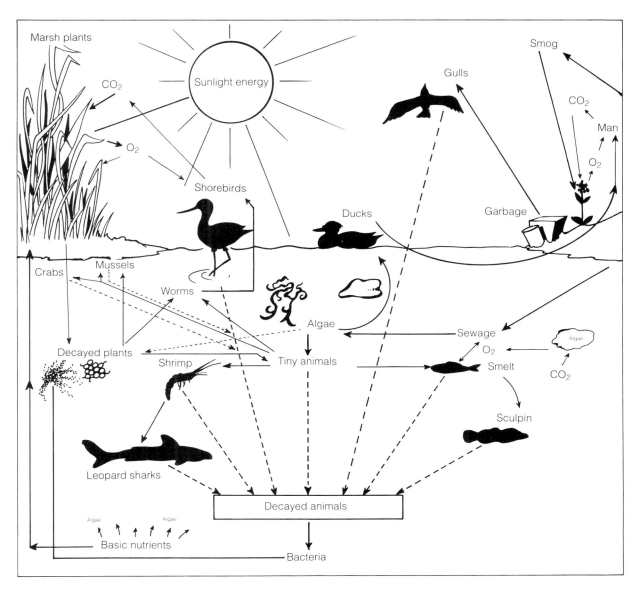

Food web and energy flow diagram

F Alternatively, work on the Bay Area tidal flats and salt-marshes could be linked to a topic on birds. Children could use additional reference material to investigate and sketch some of the common birds of the Baylands. A variety of these is shown over the page to guide further research. Compare and contrast these birds with species commonly found in our wetlands. Suggest that the children try and find out which are permanent residents and which are seasonal visitors to the Bay.

San Francisco Bay

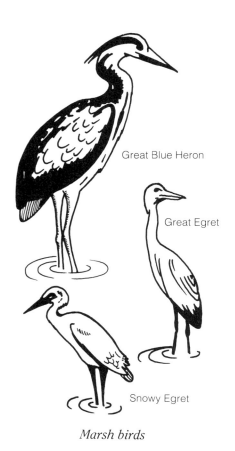

Marsh birds

Water fowl

Shorebirds

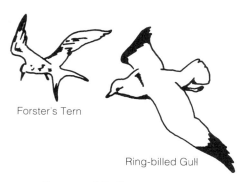

Terns and Gulls

Songbirds

Birds of prey

Activity 23: The importance of the missions

A Pursue further investigations of the importance and impact of the missions. These buildings are treasures of the Californian state which have been threatened by earthquakes and building erosion. Help the children to appreciate that these missions are significant for a number of reasons: first and foremost for their religious influence, and also for representing the continuing legacy of the impact of Spanish culture on California.

Background information
The adobe mission buildings serve as a permanent reminder of the arrival of Europeans in California. 21 missions founded by the Spanish between 1769 and 1823 still stand today in a coastal chain. Ten of these, including San Francisco de Asis, the Mission Dolores in San Francisco, are in a stable condition, whilst nine are under threat of closure and three are badly damaged. These buildings have been described as 'the Rome of California, from an architectural perspective'. The Franciscan padres who built them and established their religion along the coast of California also inaugurated a style of architecture that became typical of the southwest of the USA. By the late nineteenth century, most of the mission buildings were in ruins, but Californians revived and restored them, so that their religious impact continued to exert a strong influence. Today many committed people belong to active groups such as 'friends' of a particular mission, or mission restoration associations, and strive to raise money for restoring and conserving mission buildings.

B Paint pictures of typical mission buildings, taking account of authentic architectural style. There are four key elements of mission architecture as shown opposite.

C Find out more about adobe, the basic mission building material: this is generally sun-dried mud bricks bound with straw or ash. Adobe walls of the missions were protected only by the tiled roof and a layer of plaster whitewash. Discuss with the class the obvious fragility of this material, and the remarkable fact that a number of missions still stand today. (Mission Dolores is one of only two which still have chapels remaining.)

D Suggest that the children design posters with appropriate slogans, advertising the need for mission preservation, for example, 'Help preserve our heritage: restoration requires funds, experts and volunteers.' Statements accompanying or incorporated in these posters should explain the religious and cultural significance of the mission buildings, and good reasons for persuading people to help preserve and restore them. This activity can of course be broadened to embrace a wider discussion on heritage, artefacts and evidence which help tell us about the past, and the need to protect and conserve buildings of historic or religious significance. A painting of Mission Dolores would make an appropriate centrepiece for posters.

E With older children, discuss the controversy associated with the religious impact of the missions. Their founding father was Junipero Serra, who was later beatified by the Catholic Church, this being only one step removed from sainthood. This action resulted in continuing protests from Native Americans who see the missions as a sad reminder of forced labour, physical abuse and death by disease for many Indian tribes of the time. Indeed, statistics indicate that the Indian populations of missions were almost wiped out in the early nineteenth century. Why not organise a class debate on the beatification of Junipero Serra, with some children speaking on behalf of the Catholic religion, and others on behalf of the Native Americans?

a) Campanario:
a wall, perhaps freestanding, that holds church bells

b) Corredor:
a long, covered outside hall, supported by pillars or arches

c) Espendaña:
an ornamental false front at the main entrance

d) Reredos:
a decorated or carved screen or wall behind the main altar

San Francisco Bay

ART

Activity 24: The Golden Gate Bridge
Suggest that the children paint dramatic pictures of the Golden Gate Bridge shrouded in a typical San Francisco fog. Alternatively, create this effect by painting the bridge, then printing 'fog clouds' with shapes cut from polystyrene or potato to cover most of its structure.

Activity 25: The old and the new in San Francisco

A Use **Copymaster 6** (San Francisco — old and new) as a basis for discussing the wide variety of architectural styles found in the city. On this copymaster Victorian houses are set against a skyline of modern skyscrapers. Ask the children's opinions as to whether they like this blend of old and new. Would they prefer to live and work in an ultra-modern, streamlined building or in one of historic interest and older style? Ask them to explain the reasons for their choice. The copymaster can of course be coloured and linked to geography and English activities on the contrasts of the city. It can also be used as a basis for ideas, for creating larger pictures and paintings of the city of San Francisco, its skyline and individual buildings.

B Paint pictures of the Baylands, showing appropriate plant, bird and animal life. The large diagram of food and energy flows suggested in science activities could benefit from being accompanied by accurate drawings and paintings of the life forms depicted. The two would be very informative if displayed side by side on a classroom wall.

ENVIRONMENTAL EDUCATION

Activity 26: Threatened environments
Help the children to appreciate that the Baylands are threatened environments: they suffer from pollution and illegal dumping of wastes from industry. Organise a discussion in which the children suggest possible pollution sources. These should include:

- motor oil
- paint products
- pet wastes
- chemicals from homes and gardens.

All of the above are washed daily into gutters and drains in the streets of Bay Area communities. From there, they flow into the storm drain system and into local creeks before emptying directly into the Bay, where they harm wildlife.

Pollution sources also include wastes and chemicals from agriculture and industry, which may be directly dumped or washed off the land into the Bay by rainwater. Draw diagrams to show the passage of pollutants into Bay waters.

Activity 27: How can we prevent pollution?
Talk about ways, both real and hypothetical, in which pollution can be stopped. Actual examples of action include:

- a scheme in Santa Clara County whereby households are encouraged to minimise pollution at source, by not allowing toxic materials into the drainage system — this involves recycling schemes and sensible disposal of wastes
- active participation by Bay Area residents in a 'Restoring the Bay' campaign, involving practical conservation work and campaigning for legislation on protection.

a) Household and garden wastes flow down drains

b) Storm drains flow into creeks and rivers

c) Rivers flow into the marshes and the Bay

The Bay Area, California, USA

San Francisco Bay C1

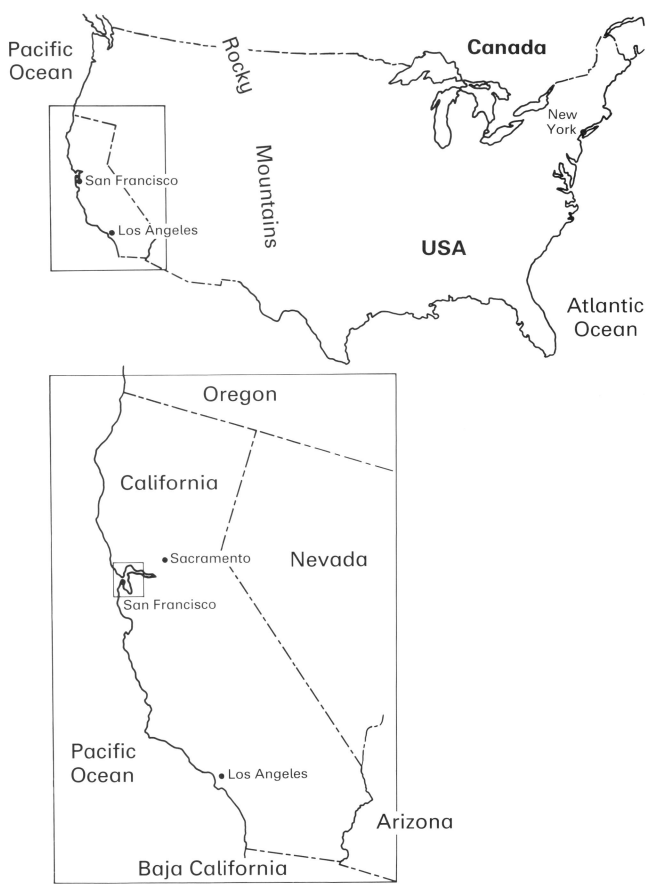

The San Francisco Bay Area

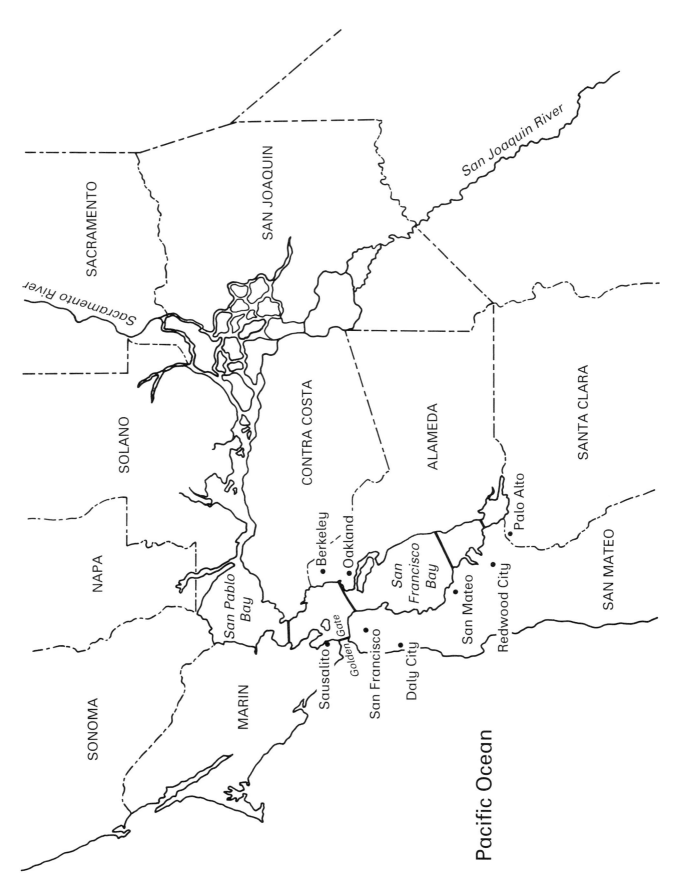

The Golden Gate Bridge

San Francisco Bay

Portraits of San Francisco

San Francisco Bay

The San Francisco Bay

San Francisco Bay

Zones of the tidal mud-flat

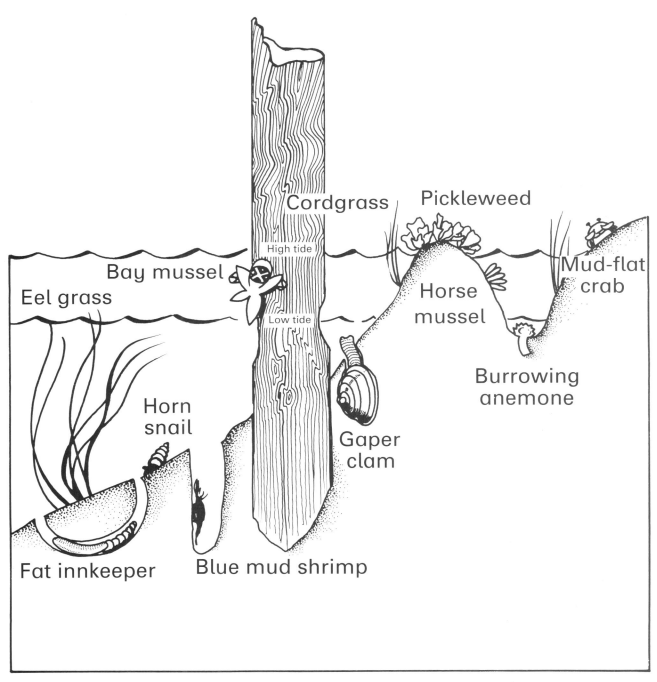

San Francisco Bay

San Francisco — old and new

HAWAII

Geography
- Location of Hawaiian Islands
- Island distances
- Born from a volcano
- Landmarks of Oahu
- The streets of Waikiki
- The importance of tourism
- Plan a holiday in Hawaii
- Hawaiian weather
- Natural hazards
- Case study of a hurricane
- Hawaiian economy today

English
- Aloha display
- Hawaiian language
- Welcome to Hawaii
- Description of island chiefs
- Story of two missionaries — a case study
- Life in Hawaii today

History
- Story of the Polynesian islanders
- The island high chiefs
- Influence of European monarchy
- Coronation of Kalakaua
- Artefacts as evidence
- Cook's third voyage, 1776–9
- Impact of missionaries
- Influence of immigration
- Wartime Hawaii
- The Arizona Memorial

HAWAII cross-curricular links

PE and music
- Dance the hula
- Hawaiian music
- Sea shanties/songs of the whalers

Mathematics
- Cost of a meal at a restaurant on the beach
- Supplementary menus
- The US dollar

Art
- Collage of a high priest
- Colours of Hawaii

Environmental education
- Conservation of island birds
- Impact of disasters

Hawaii

INTRODUCTION

In August 1959, the islands of Hawaii in the Pacific Ocean officially became the fiftieth state of the United States of America. These islands have a long and fascinating history. The separate land masses are actually the summits of a great volcanic mountain range that stretches some 3200 kilometres (2000 miles) across the floor of the Pacific Ocean. The main islands are called the 'High Islands'.

Polynesians from the Marquesas and Tahiti arrived on the Hawaiian islands between AD 500 and 900, bringing their families, household goods and domestic animals and plants in huge outrigger canoes. These early settlers lived a stone age life. They made grass houses, canoes and cloth, subsisting on fish, fruit and vegetables. Each island was ruled by a chief who surrounded himself with privileged courtiers or priests. For over a thousand years, the outside world made no impact upon their culture.

In January 1778, Captain Cook discovered the islands, landing two ships at Waimea on the island of Kauai. He named the islands the Sandwich Islands in honour of his patron, the Earl of Sandwich. Over a year later, when Cook returned, he was wounded in a skirmish with hostile natives and eventually stabbed to death. Sailors who returned from Cook's last voyage told of the discovery of the islands, but it was almost seven years before other British ships visited the islands.

In the 1750s, Chief Kamehameha I was born, and this marked the beginning of a great and powerful monarchy destined to rule Hawaii for almost a century. The influence of this dynasty was to be disturbed by the arrival of American and British missionaries, whalers and traders, and by 1820 a great struggle was taking place for control of the islands. The United States of America recognised Hawaii as an independent nation, but not for long: in June 1900, Hawaii was established as a territory of the USA. A huge wave of immigrants descended on the islands, which were by then flourishing in sugar and pineapple production. These new arrivals (Japanese, Spaniards, Filipinos, Koreans, Russians, Portuguese and other European nationalities) rapidly transformed Hawaii into a land of mixed races and cultures. Just over a century after the arrival of Captain Cook, indigenous Hawaiians had become a minority race on the islands.

Once annexed to the USA, Hawaii became established as the nation's chief site of defence in the Pacific. In December 1941, the Japanese attacked Pearl Harbour and other installations on the island of Oahu, marking the commencement of the USA's major involvement in the Second World War.

Following this conflict, various attempts were made to gain statehood for Hawaii. This plan received the support of the Congress of the United States in March 1959, and Hawaii officially became a state in August of that year.

Today, the Hawaiian Islands remain an ethnic melting pot. Many different cultures, races, religions, philosophies and lifestyles intermingle and blend. The semi-tropical climate enables Hawaii to thrive as a location for tourists and as a producer of agricultural goods. In order of importance, the three key aspects of the Hawaiian economy are tourism, federal defence activity and agriculture, notably the production of sugar cane and pineapple. Other significant crops are coffee, fruits and macadamia nuts.

GEOGRAPHY

Activity 1: Where are the Hawaiian Islands?
Introduce the location of the islands of Hawaii by showing the class a map of the world or a globe. In order to appreciate their isolation, as well as their fascinating geography, history, cultural diversity and present-day way of life, it is essential that children understand two basic facts:

1 The Hawaiian islands are part of the United States of America. A group of islands make up the State of Hawaii.
2 The Hawaiian islands are positioned an extremely long way from the mainland of the USA, some 3860 kilometres (2400 miles) west. Thus, they are geographically remote, surrounded by the vast Pacific Ocean.

Use **Copymaster 1** (Map of the main islands in the State of Hawaii) to teach the names of the five main islands in the state. These are (from west to east) Kauai, Oahu, Molokai, Maui, and Hawaii. Three other islands are shown on the map: suggest that the children use atlases to identify and then label these. They are Niihau, Lanai and Kahoolawe. All islands and the Pacific Ocean can be coloured and other details added, for example, names of key towns, distances between islands, and so on. Discuss the smaller map of the state included on the copymaster, pointing out that the main islands are **not** the complete state!

Background information
The State of Hawaii consists of a great deal more than most people think. Only five islands are well-known to tourists, but Hawaii includes more than 124 islands and islets, extending from Kure Island to the island of Hawaii itself. The eight familiar islands are called the High Islands, whilst the others are mostly uninhabited lava reefs and coral shoals: these are called the Leeward Islands, the Hawaiian Islands' National Wildlife Refuge. The total land area is at present 16 700 square kilometres (6 450 square miles), but this is continually on the increase as new land is formed by volcanic activity and coral accretions.

The best known island is Oahu, the site of the state capital, Honolulu, and other well-known places and landmarks. Hawaii is the island furthest to the east, and is almost twice as large as the other main islands put together: it is known as the 'Big Island'. Hawaii has the state's highest mountain (Mauna Kea, 3965 metres) and the state's only active volcanoes, Mauna Loa and Kilauea.

Distance by air (kilometres)

Honolulu–Hanalei (Kauai)	188
Honolulu–Hoolehua (Molokai)	88
Hoolehua–Lanai City	43
Lanai City–Kahului (Maui)	56
Kahului–Waimea (Hawaii)	127
Honolulu–Waimea	277
Honolulu–San Francisco	3855

The above distances can be entered on the copymaster by locating the towns, adding them to the map, and linking them by dotted lines to show the air routes. Depending on the age and ability of the children, these figures could be used as the basis for a discussion of scale and, perhaps, to generate some Hawaiian mathematics: routes between the islands could be planned and children asked to calculate distances travelled by 'island hoppers'.

Activity 2: What are volcanic islands?
Help the children to appreciate what is meant by the term 'volcanic islands', which is an extremely abstract concept. Talk and find out more about volcanoes as a feature, their origins and impact on the Earth. As a result, ask the children to write descriptions of the origins of Hawaii which begin with the words: 'Born from volcanic fires and glowing lava...'

Activity 3: High over the volcano
A Write about what the active volcano on the island of Hawaii would look like if you flew over it in a helicopter: molten rock or lava surfacing through the vent or opening of the volcano, spilling out over the surrounding land.

B Explain that eventually volcanoes cease to be active. At various places on the volcanic Hawaiian Islands, visitors can see evidence of extinct volcanoes: Diamond Head, Waikiki, Honolulu, for example, is an extinct volcanic crater.

Background information
The surface of the earth contains several thousand volcanoes, though only around 500 or so are active to any marked degree and many of these may not have erupted for hundreds of years. Over two-thirds of the world's volcanoes can be found around the edges of the Pacific Ocean. This area is sometimes known as the 'Ring of Fire'.

When volcanoes erupt, they emit not only lava, but also gases, such as oxygen, hydrogen and chlorine, as well as water vapour, sulphur fumes, rocks and tiny particles of volcanic dust. Solid debris includes rocks, dust particles and solidified lava: these are known as pyroclastics and in time, they form volcanic hills around the site of the volcano.

Activity 4: The island of Oahu
A Use **Copymaster 2** (The island of Oahu) to lead into discussion and further investigation of some of Hawaii's best known places and landmarks. This copymaster has deliberately been drawn without labels, so that it can serve a variety of purposes. Children could individually research aspects of the island of Oahu (brochures obtained from travel agents are an excellent source of basic information, which can be supplemented by more detailed books on the USA) and add significant features of their own choice to their copymaster, perhaps designing a suitable key as they go along. Alternatively, children could be set the challenge of locating and finding out more about a number of specified places, such as Pearl Harbour, Honolulu, Waikiki, Diamond Head and Haleiwa. These sites are shown below, together with a brief statement overleaf about each for the benefit of teachers wishing to give a specific focus to Oahu studies. The children could be divided into groups, with each group studying one of these named features: results could be combined into a book on Oahu or, perhaps, a computerised database on the Hawaiian Islands.

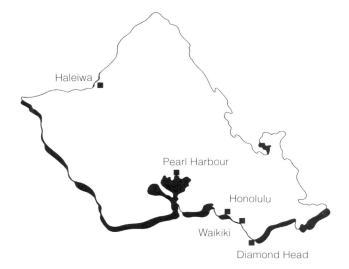

The island of Oahu

Hawaii

Background information

Pearl Harbour is a name synonymous with tragedy to the people of the USA. It lies in the west of Honolulu, in the estuary of the Pearl River, and was the site of the Japanese attack on the US navy during the Second World War (December 1941). Pearl Harbour functioned as a Pacific naval base throughout the war and is still engaged in defence activities, being a naval shipyard, a supply centre and a submarine base.

Honolulu is the capital city of the State of Hawaii. It has a population of 325 000, consisting of a great variety of nationalities, including many thousands of Japanese. The name *Honolulu* means 'protected harbour.' the heart of the old town centre is the harbour, which receives fishing boats, freight ships and large liners. There are extensive banking, commercial and shopping districts and numerous skyscrapers, giving visitors an impression of a thriving, ultra-modern city, rather than a holiday resort on a Pacific island.

Waikiki is the tourist resort of Honolulu, to the east of the city. It has a magnificent shoreline of golden beaches, backed by high-rise hotels, and busy, bustling streets lined with restaurants, souvenir shops and supermarkets catering for the needs of holidaymakers. Waikiki is discussed further in Activity 5.

Diamond Head is a 232-metre-high extinct volcanic crater in Waikiki, probably the most famous landmark on Oahu. The name derives from the volcanic crystals that sailors of the nineteenth century mistook for diamonds.

Haleiwa was the site of the first missionary church on the north coast of the island. Today it is well known as a tourist resort and as a harbour for deep sea fishing boats.

B Identify and label the main peaks of the volcanic mountains. These are shared between two ranges: the Aianae Range in the west with Kaala (1234 metres), Puu Kaua (954 metres) and Palikea (945 metres); and the Koolau Range in the east with Eleao (809 metres), Puu Kawipoo (745 metres), and Puu Konahuanui (961 metres).

C Shade and label some of the well-known beaches of the island, including Waikiki Beach, Koko Head, Halona Cove, Makapuu Beach, Waimea Bay Beach, Sunset Beach, Ala Moana Beach, Hanauma Bay Beach, Kaiona Beach and Hauula Beach. (Note that the island has 63 beaches, so only the main ones can be shown.)

Activity 5: More about Waikiki

Find out more about the most popular tourist resort in the state: Waikiki, in Honolulu. Use **Copymaster 3** (Street map of Waikiki) as a basis for discussing the geography of Waikiki and the origins of some of its well-known streets. First, discuss the location of the bustling streets of Waikiki, between the ocean and the Ala Wai Canal. (Note that only some of the main streets of the town are shown — the copymaster is a simplified version.) The canal acts as a natural barrier, enclosing the town in a relatively small area (2.4 kilometres east–west). Within this built-up district, three key roads run roughly parallel to the canal (Ala Wai Boulevard, Kuhio Avenue, and Kalakaua Avenue). These are some of the busiest streets and are crowded with hotels, shops and restaurants. A number of other streets intersect the main three roughly at right angles, forming geometric 'blocks' within the town.

Activity 6: The street names of Waikiki

A The origins of the street names of Waikiki are closely linked to its history, and discussion on this can be on-going throughout the topic. As historical activities and research are undertaken, there will inevitably be cries of 'That's where that street name came from!' To begin with, the children will no doubt find the pronunciation of street names rather difficult, but as stories are told and language discussed, words and spellings should become familiar.

B Use the copymaster as the basis for practising understanding of geographical concepts such as direction. Children could play direction games in pairs, where one gives orders (e.g. 'start at the beach, walk up Lewers Street and turn right at Kalakaua. What is the first street you come to on the map?') and the other provides the correct answer.

C If brochures can be obtained from travel agents, these usually give precise locations of named hotels, which can then be added to the map with a key to bring it to life.

D Enlarge the map by drawing it on to the classroom wall, and annotate it with illustrations of hotels cut from travel brochures and attached in their correct locations.

E Ask the children to suggest why Hawaii is such a popular resort for tourists. They will no doubt comment on its warm weather, beautiful beaches and popular image as a paradise, providing idyllic islands for a 'get-away-from-it-all' holiday.

Activity 7: Plan a Hawaiian holiday

Plan a holiday to Hawaii. This activity is best undertaken in groups: each group could plan a complete two-week holiday, using information derived from travel brochures and tourist information books. Provide each group with a checklist of things they will need to research and document, and individuals could, perhaps, focus on different aspects, such as:

- their chosen destination (island, resort, hotel)
- details of the journey (dates, airports, times)
- cost of the holiday (hotel and air package, food, recreation, insurance, etc.)
- documents needed (passport)
- details of what they may do whilst they are on holiday (local places of interest, recreation facilities, etc.)
- a check list for packing (including plenty of sunblock... and an umbrella!).

All of these details and information can be assembled in 'Hawaiian Holiday' books by each group.

Activity 8: The weather in Hawaii

A Find out more about the weather of the islands. Draw graphs of typical maximum and minimum temperatures in various places, based on the information provided below. This activity will confirm that Hawaii is a very pleasant place to be at all times of the year, at least as far as temperature is concerned. Further graphs could be drawn which show comparative statistics of Hawaii and London, or elsewhere in Britain.

Background information

Average Maximum/Minimum Temperatures (°C) and Rainfall (cms) From the records of the National Weather Service												
	JAN.	FEB.	MAR.	APR.	MAY	JUNE	JULY	AUG.	SEP.	OCT.	NOV.	DEC.
HAWAII												
Hilo, Hawaii	26.7	26.1	26.1	26.7	27.2	28.3	28.3	28.9	28.9	28.3	27.2	26.1
	17.2	17.2	17.2	18.3	18.9	19.4	20.0	20.0	20.0	19.4	18.9	17.8
	22.9	33.0	35.6	33.0	27.9	17.8	25.4	27.9	17.8	27.9	35.6	40.6
Honolulu, Oahu	26.1	26.1	26.7	27.2	28.9	30.0	30.6	30.6	30.6	30.0	28.3	26.7
	18.3	18.3	18.9	20.0	21.1	22.2	22.8	23.3	22.8	22.2	21.1	19.4
	10.2	5.1	7.6	2.5	2.5	0.0	2.5	2.5	2.5	5.1	7.6	10.2
Kahului, Maui	26.7	26.1	26.7	27.8	28.9	30.0	30.0	30.6	30.6	30.0	28.3	26.7
	17.8	17.8	17.8	18.9	19.4	20.6	21.1	21.7	21.1	20.6	20.0	18.9
	10.2	7.6	7.6	2.5	2.5	0.0	0.0	0.0	0.0	2.5	5.1	7.6
Lihue, Kauai	25.6	25.6	25.6	26.1	27.2	28.3	28.9	29.4	29.4	28.3	27.2	25.6
	17.8	17.8	18.3	19.4	21.1	22.2	22.8	23.3	22.8	21.7	21.1	19.4
	15.2	10.2	12.7	7.6	5.1	5.1	5.1	5.1	5.1	10.2	15.2	15.2

In this semi-tropical climate, temperature seldom varies more than 13 degrees Celsius. Highs range from 24–30 degrees Celsius (mid-70s to mid-80s Fahrenheit) and lows range from 17–21 degrees Celsius (mid-60s to low-70s Fahrenheit). The islands tend to be very wet places, especially in certain spots. The wettest place on earth is Mount Waialeale in Kauai. The annual rainfall of Kauai as a whole is usually around 125 centimetres, resulting in lush green vegetation and its nickname 'The Garden Isle'.

B Whilst this climate may sound idyllic, the children should understand that geographical features and processes make the Hawaiian island susceptible to many natural hazards including hurricanes, tidal waves (*tsunami*) and earthquakes. Prepare a large wall display, divided into two major sections, perhaps with a map of the islands in the centre. On the left-hand side, write about and illustrate aspects of the beauty and idyllic nature of 'paradise islands'. On the right-hand side, write about and illustrate the range of hazards which may strike at any time without warning.

Hawaii: The beauty and the dangers

Hawaii

Background information

The origins and dangers of earthquakes are fully discussed in the topic on San Francisco Bay (pages 42–5). Hurricanes are tremendously heavy storms of rain and wind. If one approaches, the National Weather Service issues a warning to leave beaches and low-lying areas and seek shelter in buildings on high ground, safe from flooding. Such warning may have little effect against the forces of nature, as the case study below demonstrates. Giant tidal waves or *tsunami* can be caused by local or offshore earth tremors, and are not always predictable: they are extremely dangerous and can wreck buildings with their force. Earthquakes are natural warnings that tidal waves will occur shortly: if a tidal wave is predicted, people should leave beaches and head for an area safe from flooding.

Activity 9: Hurricane Iniki

A Tell the story of and discuss what has been described as the worst disaster ever to hit Hawaii. This was the hurricane which devastated the island of Kauai in September 1992. Whilst it happened in the very recent past, this event will become well established in the history of the state, and serve as a permanent reminder that the apparently ideal weather conditions associated with the Hawaiian Islands can change dramatically from time to time. The following background material provides the facts of the event and remarks made at the time by local people. This material is intended to be shared with the children in a variety of ways: facts can be told and discussed; quotations can be read out; or they can be written on cards, so that the children can read and refer to them, piece together the whole story, and retell it in their own words.

Background information

On Friday 11 September 1992, Hurricane Iniki hit the island of Kauai, Hawaii. It roared through the island, smashing its way through homes and holiday hotels, ripping roofs off buildings, overturning cars and uprooting trees. The storm winds raged at speeds of up to 280 kilometres (175 miles) per hour. Three days later, it was reported that three people had died in the devastation, that 8000 of the 50 000 islanders were homeless, and that the cost of the disaster was estimated at £2 billion. Officials on the scene reported that giant waves smashed through the windows of houses and hotels, rocks and boulders were hurled into buildings, and furniture and household goods were washed away. Power, water and telephone services were destroyed, hotels closed, and thousands of holidaymakers sought shelter in emergency accommodation set up in public buildings and school halls.

Hurricane Iniki was the strongest storm to hit Hawaii this century. Inevitably, the airport was closed and for a time the island had little contact with the outside world. Red Cross volunteers camped out in airport hotel lobbies, waiting for news of transport to and from the island. Coastal vessels ferried essential supplies and US Marine helicopters flew in navy medical doctors to assist the injured.

The President of the USA declared Kauai a federal disaster area: only military supply planes were allowed to land.

What the people said:

> I saw total devastation. Our beautiful island is devastated. It broke my heart.
> (Mayor Yukimura of Kauai)

> One in every two or three homes has been destroyed or badly damaged. There isn't a pane of glass left on the island.
> (Federal disaster agency official)

> The damage is so extensive, I don't know how to describe it. At this point, it's a question of identifying homes which are still standing. This is probably the worst disaster we have had in the State of Hawaii.
> (Mr John Waihee, Governor of Hawaii)

B A variety of activities can relate to this story. Ask the children to imagine that they are news reporters on the scene in Kauai, telling the story with dramatic headlines (e.g. 'Hawaiian Havoc', 'Hurricane Wrecks Hawaii's Beautiful Isle', 'Worst Disaster Hits Paradise Island'). Alternatively suggest that they tell the story from the viewpoint of various different parties involved. Individual children could, perhaps, take on different roles, writing about, for example, the disaster as seen by a resident, a holidaymaker, a hotelier, a military doctor, a pilot, the Governor of Hawaii and the President of the USA.

Activity 10: Newspaper reports

Design and construct a newspaper front-page feature on the disaster. This could be mounted as a wall display, with contributions from different individuals and groups, including the headlines, the story, facts of the disaster, quotations from local people, illustrations and a map showing the location of Kauai.

Activity 11: The Hawaiian economy

Discuss the present-day economy of the Hawaiian Islands, which owes a great deal to the semi-tropical climate. The three major contributors to island wealth are (in order of priority) tourism, federal defence activity and agriculture. The class could paint or make a collage display, showing the islands surrounded by pictures (perhaps cut from magazines) of the main agricultural goods. This could be followed by an investigation of the conditions necessary for the growth of these plants and of how they are grown and harvested.

Hawaii

A Hawaiian harvest

HISTORY

Activity 12: The history of Hawaii
Explain to the class and discuss with them the fascinating history of the islands of Hawaii. When the first Europeans arrived, Hawaiian history was already more than 1000 years in the making. Suggest the comparison with European history, which is that little more than 200 years have gone by since the days of explorers such as Cook, Vancouver and La Perouse. An understanding of the early years of these islands' history is essential for an appreciation of the cultural diversity of today.

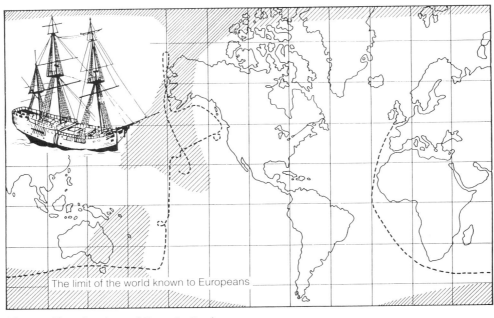

The world at the time of Captain Cook

Hawaii

Background information

When the first Europeans and Americans arrived, they found a people whose politics, arts and culture were all well established. After several decades of inter-island warfare, Hawaii was on the verge of unification under a single high chief. To the Polynesians, the native people of Hawaii, the islands' royal chiefs were descendants of their gods. The highest chiefs exerted fierce control over the people beneath them: they were infused with *mana*, the spiritual power of highborn ancestry, which established their claims to authority. Pride and power were associated with genealogies: the longest ancestral chains of the high priests went back over 100 generations. The highest of chiefs were well known. Sacred *kapus*, the sanctified laws, forbade any contact with commoners: should any commoner fall within 'the shadow' of a high priest, then death was the penalty.

During the ceremonies or in battle, the chiefs wore spectacular coloured cloaks and other attire. Bright feathers from the native forest birds of the islands were collected and tied to a mesh of woven forest vines to form a cloak. The rank of a chief was indicated by the colours of the feathers used.

Gradually through the years, the chiefs of the islands began to assume the trappings and titles of royalty. During the nineteenth century, when kings were held in awe in other parts of the world, the idea of the Hawaiian monarchy became well established. The Royal Family of Britain was not without considerable influence, and by the time of the reign of chief Kamehameha III (1825–54), a flavour of 'Victoriana' could be identified: the chief was proclaimed a king, and the feathered helmet was replaced by a golden crown. The king had a royal court of princes and princesses, and feathered cloaks were replaced by European-style military uniforms. Victorian fashions soon became the norm for the new queens and princesses. Only a few ancient native traditions, such as the carrying of *Kahili* (tall bone-and-wood standards) by the highborn chiefs, survived these new fashions.

European trappings were certainly evident in the reign of Kealakekua (1874–91). Otherwise known as the 'Merry Monarch', Kealakekua had built a Victorian-style palace for himself and his royal court. In 1833, on the ninth anniversary of his election to the throne, he staged an elaborate coronation for himself and Queen Kapiolani.

In 1893, Queen Liliuokalani was overthrown and Sanford B. Dale was appointed by the USA at the head of a provisional government. Agitation for Hawaii to become annexed to the USA had developed and reached a climax, especially as the islands' economy thrived through sugar production. In 1894, a republic was declared by the Hawaiian Legislature and on 14 June 1900 Hawaii was established as a Territory of the USA. Once annexed, the islands became the USA's chief site of Pacific defence, and are famous for the Japanese attack on Pearl Harbour on 7 December 1941.

Hawaii officially became a state of the USA (the last of the present 50) on 21 August 1959.

Although the Hawaiian monarchy no longer exists, to this day there is still a very real respect on the islands for those of highborn lineage.

Activity 13: How do we know about the Hawaiian high chiefs?

Discuss the nature of the historic evidence we have of the appearance and ways of life of the royal high chiefs. A very important source of evidence is the testimony of contemporary eyewitnesses (e.g. the words of David Schnell, recorded under the section of English activities).

Activity 14: Case study of a Hawaiian chief

Following on from the above discussion, suggest that the children focus on one historic chief and prepare a case study, including accurate descriptions and illustrations, and stating how we know such things to be accurate. Other reference material could be consulted for this purpose, but the following information on Chief Kamehameha the Great will be useful.

Background information

Kamehameha the Great, who rose to power in 1782, is today honoured by statues in Honolulu and on the 'Big Island' of Hawaii. The Honolulu statue depicts him wearing the *Ke'ei kapu o Liloa*. This was the most sacred symbol of royal power, a huge cummerbund-like sash made in 1475 on the order of King Liloa who had it made for his son, Umii. The name *Ke'ei kapu o Liloa*, literally translated, means 'the sacred sash of Liloa'. The sash, measuring some $3\frac{1}{2}$ metres in length, was draped over the chief's shoulder and wrapped around the waist. It was covered in feathers on both sides and was edged with rows of human and fish teeth. Today, the sash lies in the Bishop Museum in Honolulu.

Kamehameha the Great also wore a *mamo* cloak, named after the mamo birds from whose feathers it was made. A US newspaper report of 1839, describing the cloak, is shown below:

> ... the value of the cloak would equal that of the purest diamonds in the several European regalia, and including the price of the feathers, not less than a million dollars worth of labour was expended upon it, at the present rate of computing wages.

Activity 15: From a chief to a king

Ask the children to write critical accounts of the influence of European monarchy on the developments in Hawaii, perhaps calling these accounts 'From Chiefdom to Royalty'. Introduce the type of evidence that enables us to understand such influence, notably the changes in costume, the building of the Iolani Palace by King Kalakaua and his coronation within it.

Activity 16: The coronation of a Hawaiian king

In addition to factual accounts of European influence and the course of events in Hawaii, the late nineteenth century also provides splendid scope for creative and imaginative writing. Suggest, for example, that children describe the coronation of Kalakaua and his spectacular palace.

Background information

Kalakaua's palace was completed in 1882, its splendour in keeping with the finest of world monarchy, including a glorious throneroom and decor, and chandeliers. The king crowned himself under a bandstand in the palace grounds, while attendant Hawaiians wore traditional royal regalia to the colourful and historic ceremony. A grand *luau* (a feast: see English activities) and dancing of the *hula* were integral to the celebration, in which the old, traditional Hawaii mingled with the influence of Europe.

Activity 17: Hawaiian artefacts as historical evidence
Discuss with the class the great importance of artefacts as historical evidence. Anyone fortunate enough to visit Honolulu would be able to see for themselves many significant objects from its history. The Iolani Palace is a splendid example, with the on-going restoration of its famous throneroom. The Bishop Museum, built by Charles Bishop in honour of his wife Bernice Pauahi, the only grandchild of Kamehameha, houses a spectacular collection of Hawaiian and Pacific island artefacts. It has, for example, 12 of the 54 long feathered capes of the chiefs known to exist, the *Ke'ei kapu o Liloa*, King Kalakaua's crown and sceptre, and many other trappings of the nineteenth-century monarchy. For children of primary school age, such things may sound very remote, being housed in a museum many thousands of miles away, yet this is a wonderful opportunity to discuss how nations (including our own) depend on artefacts and museums for evidence of their past; and indeed how, with modern transport, the artefacts of Hawaii are easily accessible to us. Given available time and money, we could be at the Bishop Museum in Honolulu in less than 24 hours.

Note that an important aspect of the history of Hawaii in the nineteenth century was the arrival and impact of missionaries from New England, USA. In November 1819 a company of missionaries left Boston Harbour for Hawaii, expecting to meet strong resistance from King Kamehameha and his priesthood. In fact, they found a very receptive people. This aspect of history is dealt with more fully in a case study of two missionaries in Activity 24.

Activity 18: Immigrants in Hawaii
Suggest that the children write accounts of the great influence of immigrants who flocked to the sugar plantations of Hawaii in the mid-1800s, and to the pineapple industry in the early twentieth century. Chinese, Japanese, Filipino, Spanish, Russian, Korean and Portuguese were amongst the races to establish themselves. Their impact was tremendous in terms of determining cultural history: soon indigenous Hawaiians were in the minority. This melting pot of racial mixes remains a feature of Hawaii today.

Activity 19: Hawaii during the Second World War
Find out more about the role of Hawaii in the development of events during the Second World War. Tell the children about the significance of the Japanese bombing of Pearl Harbour in 1941. Use **Copymaster 4** (The Arizona Memorial) as a starting point for discussion and writing.

Background information
The USS Arizona Memorial commemorates all the servicemen of the USA who were killed during the 1941 attack on Pearl Harbour and it was dedicated on 30 May 1962. More than 1170 American servicemen are entombed in the sunken hull of the USS *Arizona*, which lies in Pearl Harbour. The memorial is divided into three sections: the bell room, where one of the ship's bells is mounted; the shrine room, which has engravings of the names of all those killed aboard the ship during the attack; and the assembly area from which the ship can be viewed.

ENGLISH

Activity 20: *Aloha!*
 Make an '*Aloha*' display with some Hawaiian words and their translations. Link this with discussion about the origins of the Hawaiian language, and the intermingling of native tongues used there today. English is of course spoken by a large number of people, but not without the inclusion of a number of Hawaiian words and the influence of expressions from the USA.

Background information
Hawaiian words in common usage include:
aloha   the 'hello' greeting (pronounced ah-*lo*-ha)
hula   the Polynesian dance (pronounced *hoo*-la)
lei   a flower garland (pronounced lay)
lanai   a porch or balcony (pronounced lah-*nigh*)
muumuu   a woman's dress (pronounced *moo*-moo)

B For your display, paint colourful pictures of Hawaii — the place and the people. Display these beneath the word '*Aloha!*'. Paint *leis* (strands of flowery garlands) around the edge of your display, or construct them from crepe paper flowers for a colourful 3-D effect.

Activity 21: Learn to speak Hawaiian
If children are old enough, extend the above activity by helping them to learn some words of the Hawaiian language, selected from the list below which gives translations and help with pronunciation:

Words in common use
aikane (aye-*ka*-nee)   friend
ala   (*ah*-la)   road
aloha   (ah-*lo*-ha)   greeting, love, welcome, farewell
brah   (brah)   brother, friend
hale   (*ha*-leh)   house
hauoli (how-o-lee)   happy, rejoice
hula   (*hoo*-la)   Polynesian dance

Hawaii

humuhumunukunukuapauaa (Hoo-moo-*hoo*-moo-*noo*-koo-*noo*-koo-*ah*-poo-*ah*-ah)	a kind of tiny fish
kai (*ka*-ee)	ocean
kala (*ka*-la)	money
kane (*ka*-nee)	man
kaukau (*cow*-cow)	food
keiki (*kay*-e-key)	child
lanai (lah-*nigh*)	porch
lei (lay)	garland
mahalo (ma-*ha*-loh)	thanks
maikai (*my*-kye)	good, fine
malihini (mah-lee-*hee*-nee)	newcomer
moana (moh-*ah*-nah)	ocean
muumuu (*moo*-oo-*moo*-oo)	woman's dress
nui (*noo*-ey)	big, huge, much
ono (*oh*-no)	tastes good
pali (*pah*-lee)	cliff

Phrases and greetings

Aloha kakahiaka (Ah-*low*-ha ka-ka he-*ah*-ka)	Good morning
Aloha ahiahi (Ah-*low*-ha ah-hee-*ah*-hee)	Good evening
Pehea oe? (Pe-*heh*-ah *oh*-hee)	How are you?
Maikai (*my*-kye)	I am fine
Mahalo nui (Ma-*ha*-low New-ee)	Many thanks
Hauoli la Hanau (*Ha*-oo-*oh*-lee la Ha-na-oo)	Happy Birthday
Mele Kalikimaka (*May*-lee Kah-*lee*-ke-*ma*-ka)	Merry Christmas
Hauoli Makahiki hou (Ha-oo-*oh*-lee Ma-ka-*hee*-kee-*ho*-oo)	Happy New Year

Activity 22: The people of Hawaii
Copymaster 5 (Welcome to Hawaii) will be enjoyed as a basis for discussion, especially by Key Stage 1 children who are not too young to appreciate and learn a small number of basic words from the Hawaiian native tongue. Explain that the copymaster shows a Hawaiian woman and man wearing typical colourful clothing. The lady has a flowing *muumuu*, and the man is wearing a brightly coloured *Aloha* shirt. Both wear a *lei*, a garland of native flowers around their necks. Suggest that the children colour the drawing, dressing the people in bright Hawaiian prints and labelling the *muumuu*, *Aloha* shirt and *leis*. This could be followed by writing simple sentences about people in Hawaii today. Alternatively, ask children to write a speech of welcome to a visitor, telling of the beauty and attractions of the islands.

Activity 23: A Hawaiian chief
A Suggest that the children write descriptions of a Hawaiian royal chief's appearance on a ceremonial occasion, or when going into battle (see also art activities), using correct words for the items of clothing: *'ahu' ula* (feather cloak); *mahiole* (helmet); and *ke'ei kapu o Liloa* (long sash). Encourage children to try and bring out the vibrant image thus created of the radiant glory of the colourful chiefs.

B If children are old enough to appreciate the following words, read to them (in association with the previous activity) the description below of the chief's clothing supplied by David Schnell, who travelled with Captain Cook to Hawaii on HMS *Discoverer* and HMS *Resolution* in 1779. These words could, perhaps, be written as the centrepiece for an appropriate wall display.

> The cloaks are made of fine netting with red and yellow feathers curiously worked upon them: these they have of various lengths, some coming no lower than the waist and others trailing to the ground. A more rich and elegant dress than this, perhaps the Arts of Europe have not been able to supply.

Activity 24: A tale of two missionaries
Read to the class or relate in your own words the following extract from the tale of two missionaries, David and Sarah Lyman, who left New England, USA, in 1831 bound for Hawaii. Their mission was to convert the islanders, then under the reign of King Kamehameha, to Christianity. The Lymans spent over 180 days at sea on their voyage to Hilo on the Hawaiian Islands.

Background information
On 26 November 1931, David and Sarah Lyman boarded the whaling ship *Averick* at New Bedford, USA. She was a strong, three-masted vessel, measuring some 34 metres long and 8 metres wide. *Averick* had been built to hunt whales, not to carry passengers: life on board was cramped and claustrophobic in the extreme. The journey was rough, and the missionaries suffered seasickness, as well as having to watch the crew engaged in their bloody whaling activities. After 173 days at sea, the *Averick* eventually anchored in Honolulu Harbour on 17 May 1832. A few weeks later, the Lymans set out once again on an 11-day journey to their destination, Hilo Bay on the Big Island. They found no roads and no shops, and their home was a room in the home of another couple. Hilo is noted for being the wettest place in the world: almost every day saw torrential rain. Rivers flooded and getting about proved to be very difficult indeed. Outrigger canoes were used to cross the Wailuku river as there were no bridges. This itself was a hazardous activity, as David Lyman wrote:

> Being told by the natives that it was good crossing in canoes, we went thither. It was about eight [o'clock] and quite dark. Our clothes were dripping and we must either sleep in them as they were or get home … we seated ourselves in a canoe and pushed off. At first, we glided along, but when we came where the current of the river came down with all its strength on one side and the surf beat heavily upon us from the other, the canoe was almost thrown out of the water. Once the outrigger flew up to a considerable

height and probably would have gone over entirely had there not been a number of natives in the canoe who were skillful in managing it, ... we reached the shore with our canoe half filled with water ...

Despite such difficult conditions, David and Sarah set enthusiastically about their missionary work. Sarah became very involved in work in schools where literacy was considered to be very important. When Hawaiian children learned the alphabet, they practised their letters on slates or paper, in wet sand or on large leaves. Printing presses set up by missions in Honolulu produced reading, spelling and arithmetic books, as well as New Testaments and catechisms. The missionaries also visited people in their homes to teach them the Christian way of life, and David toured the island preaching the gospel.

Home life was not easy. Food was difficult to come by, and much was imported from around Cape Horn. By the time it arrived, it was often mouldy, insect- or rat-infested, or soaked with sea water. In 1836, however, David opened and became principal of the new Hilo Boarding School, which was built with a house for the Lymans to live in. By this time, they had a family, including a son Henry who described their new house as:

> ... a wooden building of one storey, placed on a stone foundation that surrounded a spacious cellar. There were four rooms on the first [i.e. ground] floor ... a dining room and common sitting room, and my mother's bedroom, on the front side, looking out upon the ocean. Behind our mother's bedroom was a smaller bedroom for my little brother Fred and myself. Behind the dining room, opening out of a narrow passage that contained the stairs, was a small room for the storage of such articles as were used in barter with the natives for provisions; in fact, it served as my father's office and reception room for such people as came on secular business. In the rear of all was a semi-detached kitchen, with an old-fashioned open fireplace and an oven all constructed out of rough stones, bricks then being unknown in Hawaii. Upstairs were two attic bedchambers with dormer windows, from which were visible the beautiful bay and the blue ocean that filled the northwestern horizon.
>
> Furnishings were very simple. Every article was of the cheapest and plainest description, though some of the woodwork sawed out of the beautiful Hawaiian *koa* might have been very ornamental had it been polished. No carpets of any kind covered the floors, no paper the plastered walls, no blinds were at the windows, only some plain white cotton sash curtains. The sole decoration consisted of a looking glass with a gilded frame that hung in the dining room, and a few coarsely coloured lithographic cards, representing incidents in the life of Jesus.

Later, the roof was raised and four extra bedrooms added to accommodate the Lyman's growing family. David and Sarah stayed in Hilo and ran the Boarding School for the rest of their lives. Their descendants still live in Hilo.

Activity 25: Evidence about the past

The above case study is clearly very useful as a cross-reference with history activities. Discuss with the class how written sources such as the Lymans' words are a powerful source of evidence about the past. From this story a great deal can be learned about Hilo, its people and everyday life. Any number of more specific activities, such as the following, can be linked to a reading of this story.

Activity 26: The Lyman journal

Suggest that the children make a class book about the Lyman family, perhaps in the form of a diary or family album, with written accounts and illustrations of their long sea journey and life in Hilo. As part of this, or as separate activities, ask them to:

- draw or paint pictures of the *Averick* on the turbulent sea
- write accounts of the terrible 173-day journey from New Bedford to Honolulu, including details of the mixed emotions of the missionaries: determination to go on and do their Christian duty; anger at the way of life of the whalers; despair at feeling seasick and having no palatable food; and anticipation of how they would be received by the native Hawaiians
- plot on a map the voyage of the *Averick* from the east coast of the USA to Honolulu around Cape Horn. With the aid of cartridge paper soaked in cold tea overnight, it may be possible to produce some convincingly authentic charts of the period, particularly if pictures of contemporary maps can be consulted for style and detail
- draw pictures of an outrigger canoe struggling along a torrential river, and write accounts of this frightening experience

- paint a large picture of the Lyman family home into which they moved in 1839

The family home of David and Sarah Lyman in Hilo

- draw or paint imaginary pictures of rooms inside the Lyman house, based on the description given by Henry Lyman. Children could also paint the view of the ocean which might be seen from the windows
- draw portraits of David and Sarah Lyman as they exist in the imaginations of the children, setting these in painted Victorian-style frames and trying to ensure that the figures are suitably clad in Victorian garb.

Activity 27: Life in Hawaii today

Write accounts of life in Hawaii today. Read (or write out for the children to read) the following statements made by present-day residents of Honolulu. Suggest that children discuss with a partner who might have written each statement, and then complete a piece of writing, imagining that they are that person and elaborating on the statement made.

- 'I experience Oahu by lacing up my hiking shoes. I step out through the forests …'
- 'I lie on the hot golden sand, day after day of fierce sun …'
- 'As my plane heads down towards the lights of Honolulu, I am pleased to be home …'
- 'My store is always busy. Bustling tourists buy their films, their gifts, their souvenirs …'
- 'Crime on the streets of Honolulu is getting worse. Often trouble comes from lively visitors at night time …'
- 'Today I made my first *lei*. I have watched Mama do this many times …'
- 'I *hula* dance the night away …'

David and Sarah Lyman, early missionaries in Hawaii

MATHEMATICS

Activity 28: Maths — Hawaiian-style

Use **Copymaster 6** (Dinner on the beach) to introduce some intriguing mathematics, focusing on the cost of eating out at a well-known Hawaiian restaurant. This copymaster shows an authentic menu of 'Xavier's Beach Broiler' on the beach in Waikiki, Honolulu. It should stimulate and indeed warrants a great deal of discussion on various aspects of the menu.

First of all, it will need to be explained that the menu prices are in US dollars ($), although the arithmetical procedure for calculating the price of meals is clearly the same as for adding-up in our own currency. There is, of course, exciting scope for talking about the current exchange rate of dollars to sterling, and calculating the cost of the various dishes in English money.

Secondly, it is interesting to discuss with the class aspects of the American way of life in restaurants: note that all meals include a 'help yourself' selection from the salad bar, chilli, rice, fried rice and fresh pasta!

Finally, discuss what is meant by 'Daily Fresh Catch': this provides another opportunity to learn some Hawaiian words, using, perhaps, a wall display of local fish specialities and their Hawaiian names. Furthermore, children could add a named price to these: the menu states that 'the waiter will inform you of availability and price', so let the children be the waiter! Use the table over the page as a translation guideline.

The children could design and 'publish', with prices, a supplementary menu to Copymaster 6, based on the information over the page.

Activity 29: A visit to the restaurant

Further to the design of this supplementary menu, divide the children into working groups and suggest that each group goes on a visit to Xavier's Beach Broiler. Children take it in turns to be the diner and the waiter who adds up the cost. It should be presumed that each diner has dinner guests: perhaps a limit of four people per group could be imposed.

To make this an even more authentic and interesting mathematical exercise, make some US dollar bills ($1, $5, $10 and $20) out of paper and let the children exchange this 'real' money for their meals, giving them the appropriate change (correct to the nearest dollar). Then, of course, one could always delve into the realms of adding a service charge, if the children are able to cope with this. 15 per cent is the expected service charge on restaurant bills in the USA: simple sums could work this out as a tenth plus half as much again.

Fresh island fish

Opakapaka	Pink Snapper
Kaku	Barracuda
Ahi	Hawaiian Tuna
Mano	Shark
Ono	Wahoo, King Mackerel
Lehi	Silver-mouthed Snapper
A'hu	Pacific Blue Marlin
Onaga	Red Snapper
Ulcu	Grey Snapper
Ulua	Giant Trevally

ART

Activity 30: A collage of Hawaiian chiefs
Make a large wall collage depicting the ancient high chiefs of Hawaii. Remind the class that brightly coloured birds' feathers were used for the cloaks, and that the colours chosen symbolised rank: red, yellow, black and green were colours commonly used. Provide your chiefs with cloaks from brightly coloured paper cut in the shape of feathers and frayed to resemble them, a helmet and a long sash. Label the collage with the appropriate Hawaiian words for these items.

Activity 31: The colours of Hawaii
Make fabric prints of the present-day colours of Hawaii. Tropical prints of brightly coloured patterns and flower designs are made into *Aloha* wear for all the family: shirts for the men and *muumuus* for the women. Design your own *Aloha* print pattern and transfer this to fabric. Either make squares of the colours of Hawaii for display, or design pieces of fabric large enough to make garments from, which can be worn for a class assembly or presentation on the theme of the islands of Hawaii.

A Hawaiian high chief

Aloha!

Activity 32: Make yourself a *lei*
Make *lei* greetings from coloured paper flowers joined together into a garland. Dress in these for a class assembly, or performance of a *hula* dance (see PE/music activities).

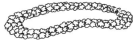

Background information
The Hawaiian Islands each have their own *leis* and colours:

Island	Colour	Flower
The Big Island	red	the red *lehua* flower
Kauai	purple	The green *mokihana* berry entwined with *maile* vine
Lanai	orange	pink and white blossoms of the *kaunaoa*
Maui	pink	the *lokelani*, a pink cottage rose
Molokai	green	the small white flower of the state tree, the *kukui*
Oahu	yellow	the yellow *ilima* flower

ENVIRONMENTAL EDUCATION

Activity 33: Fine-feathered friends
Discuss the implications of using feathers from native birds for the construction of the capes of ancient chiefs. One large cloak required the plumage from up to 80 000 birds. Explain to the class that feathers were collected by ordinary people as part of their duties to lesser chiefs. These, in turn, passed them to the higher chiefs. Some birds were 'feather harvested' and then released, but most were killed outright and all of their plumage used. Many species used in this way are now extinct, whilst others are extremely rare.

Ask the children their views on this procedure. You could hold a class debate on 'Feathers for the Chiefs', with some children putting forward the case for the chief's needs and the duties of ordinary people, and others the case for the conservation of native bird life.

Activity 34: Natural disasters
Discuss the environmental impact of natural disasters such as the hurricane of September 1992, as outlined in the geography activities. Quite apart from the costs measured in terms of lives, buildings and material goods, such disasters have a horrifying effect on the environment: rare species of native plants and wildlife are inevitably reduced or wiped out completely, and soil is washed away by flooding. It could be pointed out to the class that some scientists believe global warming is causing hurricanes to become more intense. If this is the case, places such as Hawaii have a bleak future. Find out more about global warming and its believed impact on weather patterns.

PE AND MUSIC

Activity 35: *Hula* dancing
Tell the children about *Hula* dancing; they could try to perform it.

Background information
Hula dancing conjures up images of grass-skirted ladies with swaying hips, engaged in a form of Polynesian go-go dance. In actual fact, the *hula* represents hundreds of years of Hawaiian history and culture. Some dances depict tales of the gods, chiefs and voyages of the islanders. Others are prayers or love stories. The *hula* was used to record people and events of history, in the absence of written language: the dances were, therefore, taken very seriously by the early islanders.

As Western music and instruments have influenced the evolution of the dance, it has taken on a more entertaining form. Gestures are still used to represent actions: if, for example, the outstretched hand and arm (palm facing down) make forward, wave-like movements, this represents motion such as walking. Paddling, swimming and diving are also represented by arm gestures.

Activity 36: Hawaiian music
Listen to some modern music from the islands, perhaps from recordings available at your local record library. Common instruments played are the steel guitar and the ukelele.

Activity 37: Sea shanties
Teach the children (or let them hear on record) some of the traditional sea shanties that the Lymans might have heard on their whaling ship. Shanties such as 'Johnny Come Down to Hilo', and 'Greenland Whale Fishing' (recorded by the folk group The Spinners) are good examples of these.

Map of the main islands in the State of Hawaii

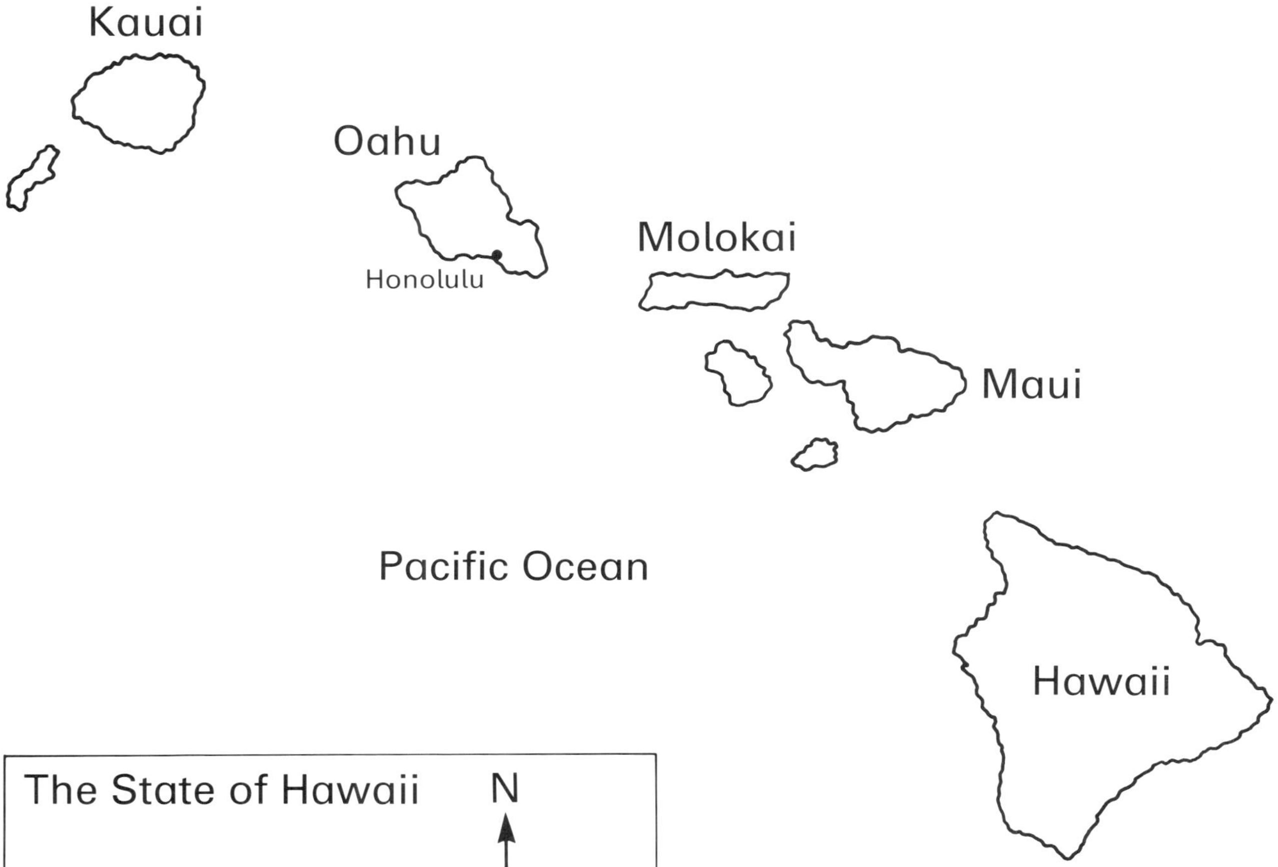

Kauai

Oahu

Honolulu

Molokai

Maui

Pacific Ocean

Hawaii

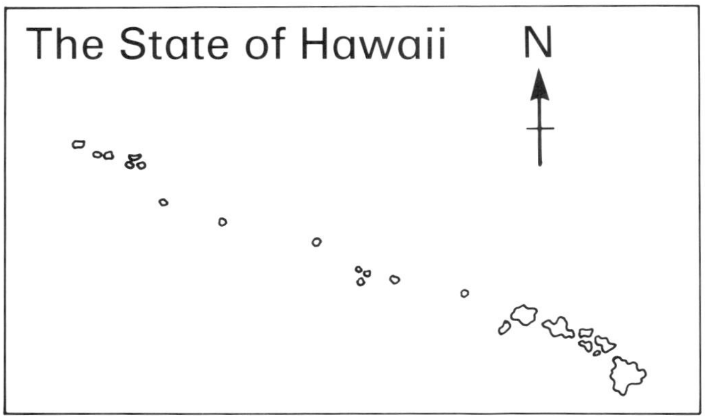

The State of Hawaii N

Hawaii

The island of Oahu

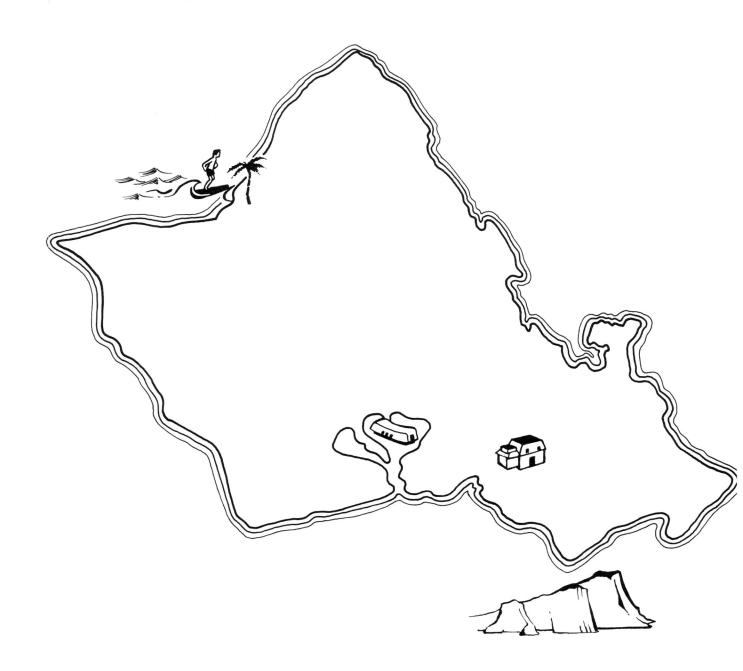

Street map of Waikiki

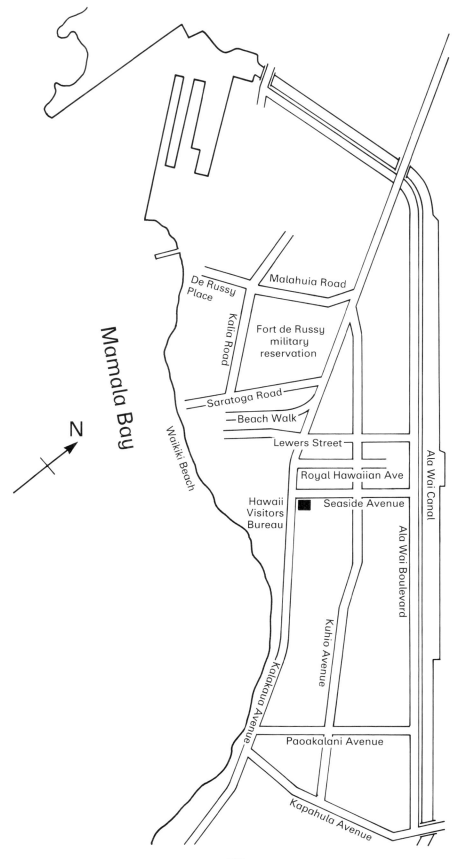

Hawaii

The Arizona Memorial

Welcome to Hawaii

Hawaii

Dinner on the beach

Complete Dinners from $7.95
All dinners include Salad Bar, Chili Rice, Fried Rice and Fresh Pasta

Baby Back Ribs $13.95	Top Sirloin $11.95
Fresh Ground Sirloin $8.95	Teriyaki Beef Kabob $11.95
Hawaiian Teriyaki Chicken (boneless) $9.95	New York Steak $14.95
	Hawaiian Teriyaki Ono $9.95
Garlic Chicken Kabob $8.95	Shrimp Kabob $12.95
Daily Fresh Catch (Your waiter will inform you of availability and price.)	Salad Bar only $5.95

SHORE BIRD SPECIAL
Island Fish Fillets (when available)... $7.95

Xavier's Beach Broiler

NEW ZEALAND

Geography
- Location of New Zealand: North and South Islands
- Geographical facts
- Lines of latitude
- New Zealand flag
- Climate: seasons of the Southern Hemisphere
- Travel to New Zealand
- Time zones, time differences
- Natural landscape
- Physical features
- Industry and economy
- Life in towns
- Tourism
- A talk by a native of New Zealand

Science
- The kiwi: origins, evolution, habits
- Kiwi family tree
- Ratites of the world today
- Non-flying bird — an oddity?
- Probing for food
- Kiwi and the Maoris
- Kiwi conservation
- Kiwi emblem
- Native trees and plants
- The cabbage tree
- Plant oddities

NEW ZEALAND cross-curricular links

History
- Polynesian navigators
- Voyage of Abel Tasman
- Explorations of Cook
- Feelings of the early settlers
- British Commonwealth status
- Development of the nation
- The Maori people — origins and tribal systems
- Decline of the Maoris
- Cultural identity, racial harmony

Art
- Maori art forms
- Tattooing
- Hakas

English
- Maori language
- Place names

New Zealand

INTRODUCTION

The country of New Zealand is made up of two main islands: North Island and South Island. They lie in the Pacific Ocean, to the south-east of Australia. New Zealand's capital, Wellington, is situated at the southern end of North Island. The native people of New Zealand are the Maoris, but the majority of the present-day population has come from Europe and elsewhere. New Zealand is a member of the British Commonwealth of Nations.

The islands of New Zealand were 'discovered' by the Dutch and claimed by the British, although the Polynesians had found the lands and settled there long before. In the seventeenth century, when several European explorers reach Australia, Abel Tasman discovered the islands of New Zealand in 1642. Many years later, in 1769, Captain Cook explored the islands. This led to the early days of emigration by British people to both Australia and New Zealand, a movement of settlers that has continued ever since. Today most of the non-indigenous people of New Zealand have come from Britain. The descendants of the Maoris mix freely with the rest of the population, whilst some retain their old customs and traditions. Thus the country represents an ideal example of the contrasts in our world between old and new, modern Western lifestyle and traditional tribal culture.

GEOGRAPHY

Activity 1: The islands of New Zealand
Use **Copymaster 1** (New Zealand: the islands), in conjunction with a world map or globe, to help children understand the location of New Zealand's two major islands in the South Pacific Ocean. Help the class to appreciate the proximity of Australia to New Zealand. The copymaster provides basic geographical information about New Zealand, which you should talk through with the children. They will see the names of the two main islands, adjacent oceans and main cities, including Wellington, the capital. Point out that the shaded area refers to land over 1000 metres in height, and that the highest mountain peaks are shown and named. The map also has a scale, so that work can be done with older children on various aspects of the country's size.

This copymaster will be of on-going use throughout the topic, as well as forming a good basis for introductory discussion. Additional information can be added as the topic progresses, such as the names of other towns, bays, the location of Stewart Island, and sites of national parks and geysers (see later activities). Younger children will enjoy colouring the ocean area in blue, the land in green and mountainous areas in brown, as a useful way of helping them to appreciate these conventional map colours. Perhaps a series of questions based on the copymaster could be produced on illustrated sheets. The example opposite could be adapted for use, depending on the ability of the pupils involved.

There is also scope for additional questions based on the use of the scale, such as the approximate width of each island, of the Cook Strait, and so on. Older children can be asked to use atlases to find out more about the precise location of New Zealand in relation to other lands, notably the USA and the Antarctic.

Background information
New Zealand lies in the South Pacific Ocean, some 2090 kilometres (1300 miles) from Australia across the

We can learn a great deal about a country from a map.

Use Copymaster 1 to help answer the following questions:

1 What are the two large islands called?
2 What is the name of the stretch of water between the islands?
3 Name the capital city of New Zealand.
4 Name the two largest towns on the South Island.
5 What is the range of mountains called?
6 How high is the highest mountain peak?
7 What is the highest peak called?
8 What is the total length of the two islands, from north to south?

Tasman Sea (note that it will be necessary to explain to children that the Tasman Sea is part of a more extensive ocean) and around 10 460 kilometres (6500 miles) from the west coast of the USA. In the south, New Zealand is only 2574 kilometres (1600 miles) from the Antarctic Circle. The country measures approximately 1600 kilometres (1000 miles) from north to south, and 306 kilometres (190 miles) across at its widest point. The coastline around the two islands measures about 6920 kilometres (4300 miles) and the area is roughly twice the size of England.

The two main islands of New Zealand are separated by the Cook Strait, which measures only 18 kilometres (11 miles) across at its narrowest point. Apart from the North and South Islands, there are hundreds of much smaller ones: the largest of these is Stewart Island, separated from South Island by the Foveaux Strait.

New Zealand

A range of mountains runs down most of the length of the country, with three key peaks: Mt Cook (3764 metres) and Mt Aspiring (3036 metres), both on South Island; and Mt Ngauruhoe (2291 metres), the highest peak on North Island.

Activity 2: What does a map of New Zealand not tell us?
Ask the children to suggest what a map of New Zealand *cannot* tell us about the country. This is a fascinating question for children, which in many ways helps to reinforce the value of maps as sources of information, whilst also helping children appreciate that there are aspects of a country that maps cannot reveal, for example, what the people, homes and weather are like, what animals and birds live there, and so on. This question will lead on to many other facets of the topic.

Copymaster 2 (Flying the flag in the Southern Hemisphere) goes some way towards linking the aspects of the land depicted by a map with the 'unseen' features, as mentioned above. This copymaster is designed to show three things: a map of New Zealand, with three key lines of latitude indicated; the flag of the country; and a globe indicating a comprehensive set of lines of latitude. In the first instance, use the copymaster to help teach about lines of latitude in general; then consider the position of New Zealand on the globe, in terms of its latitude and location in the Southern Hemisphere; then talk about the flag of New Zealand, and the fact that the country is a member of the British Commonwealth of Nations.

This copymaster should be used in conjunction with a globe, letting children compare the small globe on the sheet with 3-D globe, and find the lines of latitude on the latter. This will then help them to locate the precise position of New Zealand in the Southern Hemisphere, south of the equator. The map on the copymaster can be used for any desired purpose; other towns could, perhaps, be located, so that their approximate latitude can be established. The flag should of course be coloured accurately, and the origin of its design researched.

Background information
Think of the Earth as a sphere or ball, which is constantly spinning. Two points remain still, the North and South Poles. Exactly halfway between the poles, running around the centre of the Earth, is an imaginary line called the equator. All places north of the equator are in what is known as the Northern Hemisphere, and all places south of the equator are in the Southern Hemisphere. Either side of the equator and parallel to it are a series of imaginary lines, like rings, circling the globe. These are lines of latitude, and are used to show how far north or south of the equator any particular place is. They are numbered from 0 (degrees) at the equator to 90 (north or south) at the poles. The children will be able to see from the copymaster that New Zealand is in the Southern Hemisphere, some 35–50 degrees south.

Activity 3: Latitudes
Look up the latitudes of other places known to the children, such as London, New York, and so on, and make comparisons with New Zealand. (Wellington is on approximately the same latitude in the Southern Hemisphere as New York is in the Northern.)

Activity 4: Latitude and climate
Relate latitude to climate. With younger children, explain in the simplest terms that, generally speaking, the nearer you are to the equator, the warmer it is. This is why the so-called hot, tropical lands are situated in bands stretching some way north and south of the equator. With older children, this activity can be usefully linked to science, and such matters as the tilting of the Earth, the passage of the Earth around the sun and the resulting seasons of the year (which differ according to the hemisphere you are in) can be considered.

The following diagram may be useful as teacher resource material, or for adapting into an appropriate form for the children. The purpose of this activity in the present context is, of course, to consider differences in the annual climate between New Zealand and the UK. Pupils should be helped to appreciate that when we are enjoying summer, it is winter in New Zealand, and vice-versa.

Background information
Note that the Earth is drawn at a tilt, at 23.5 degrees on its axis: this is why we have seasons. The diagram shows how the Earth moves around the sun. The hot season occurs when the sun is high in the sky over a country and the cold season when the sun is low. When the sun is high in the sky in New Zealand (December), it is low in the sky in the UK. The midday sun is overhead at the equator in March and September, and at the tropic of Cancer in June and the tropic of Capricorn in December.

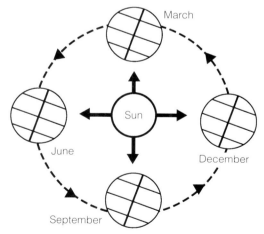

The seasons of the year

Activity 5: Temperature around the world
Obtain a series of daily newspapers which provide temperature statistics of various places in the world, and keep a record of these. Compare statistics for Wellington to those of London, or your home town. Draw graphs of daily temperatures in Wellington over a period of time: again, comparative graphs can be drawn for London and elsewhere. Use the newspapers to

New Zealand

research which other places in the world are having similar temperatures to New Zealand at any particular time of year.

Background information
Apart from at the highest mountain peaks, New Zealand has a fairly even climate, with no extremes of temperature. In the south (Dunedin) the winter temperature falls to freezing, but elsewhere winters are generally mild. Rainfall varies from some 635 centimetres per year at Milford Sound in the south-west to 30 centimetres in parts of central Otago. Most of the country receives between 76 and 127 centimetres of rain per year.

Activity 6: How can you get to New Zealand?
Find out how to get to New Zealand. Try and enlist the help of a travel agent, who may willingly supply the class with details of airlines which fly there from the UK, flight times and other modes of transport, for example, by ocean liner. Find out the speediest route from the UK to New Zealand together, perhaps, with the longest route in terms of time taken to travel; also find out the least expensive route.

Activity 7: A flight to New Zealand

A On a world map, plot the journey of an aircraft flying east from the UK to New Zealand. Note details of countries over which the plane would pass, and possible stops it may make en route. Ask the children to consider whether a passenger would cross the equator during the journey. Would they be able to see it?

B Write stories entitled 'Journey Down Under', describing landscapes and places in the world that might be seen from an aeroplane window during the long journey east to the other side of the world.

C Consider alternative routes, perhaps flying west across the United States and via the Hawaiian Islands. The above activity could be repeated for this flight path.

Activity 8: Time zones
When discussing flight times and durations of journeys, talk about the time difference between the UK and New Zealand. New Zealand is 12 hours ahead of Greenwich Mean Time. Help the children to appreciate the fact that because New Zealand is on the opposite side of the world, day time here means night time there. This activity could be linked to some interesting mathematics. Devise some work cards showing UK time, and ask the children to calculate the equivalent New Zealand time, which should prove to be a relatively easy task on a 12-hour clock. More complex mathematics can be introduced by giving your times on a 24-hour clock.

Activity 9: The landscape of New Zealand
Collect as many resource materials as possible, including reference books, travel agency brochures and posters, to enable the children to find out as much as possible about the natural landscape of New Zealand. Ask them to share their images of the country with the rest of the class, and develop this into a discussion, leading on to writing about and drawing pictures of the natural beauty of this land.

Background information
Much of New Zealand is unspoilt natural landscape, with mountains, valleys, glaciers, lakes and forests. The coastline is also extensive and beautiful, with numerous beaches and bays. In places, the mountains appear to rise almost out of the sea, providing spectacular scenery. Elsewhere, agricultural countryside dominates the landscape, with mile after mile of fields and hedgerows, similar to an English rural scene.

Activity 10: Words about New Zealand
Discuss and perhaps organise a quiz on geographical vocabulary applicable to New Zealand, asking the children to find out what particular words mean and, perhaps, to find pictures in travel books illustrating these features. A class dictionary could be compiled as a result of this activity, with illustrated entries provided by individual children or groups. Words to include in this dictionary are shown in the artwork below.

Note that New Zealand has active volcanoes and much evidence of past volcanic activity. Hot spas, mineral springs and geysers are great tourist attractions.

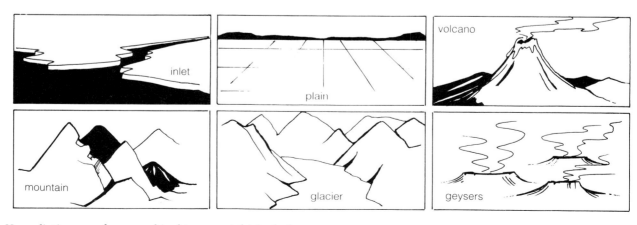

Your dictionary of geographical terms might include...

Activity 11: The New Zealand way of life

A Once again, additional reference material will need to be collected in order to help children find out about general ways of life in New Zealand, in both town and country, and about key features of the nation's economy. Depending on the age of the children, some initial help may be given, for example, by organising the class into groups, with each group researching one of the aspects shown below, and given available pictures and reference materials. With younger children, simple sentences could be provided helping them to appreciate that the elements below are all important to the economic life of New Zealand. A collage wall display could be built up, based on the artwork.

B Use travel agency brochures alongside reference books to find out about New Zealand towns, their architecture, well-known buildings and general characteristics. Almost half of the population lives in four cities: Auckland, Wellington, Christchurch and Dunedin. Most people live in single-storey houses, so housing takes up a lot of space and cities tend to sprawl over a huge area. Most cities were founded by settlers from Britain who migrated under schemes organised by such corporations as the New Zealand Company, which founded Wellington.

Activity 12: Tourism in New Zealand

Research the impact and extent of tourism in New Zealand by using holiday brochures. These will give a clear indication of the most popular tourist 'hot spots'. Suggest that the children discuss photographs of tourist attractions provided by a range of brochures whilst considering their descriptions; then cut out a set of pictures of places they would like to visit, together with accompanying information.

This can be collected together and compiled as a class book of New Zealand tourist attractions. Ask each child to tell the class about the place or feature of the country he or she would most like to visit, and explain why. See if any consensus of opinion emerges on New Zealand's greatest attractions.

Activity 13: A visitor from New Zealand

If possible, find a person who has lived in or visited New Zealand, and who would be prepared to talk to the class about his or her impressions of the country. If you are fortunate enough to contact such a person, work with the class to structure an interview, rather than merely asking him or her to come and talk about New Zealand, which could lead to a complex, unstructured mass of unrelated information being given. Decide what you want to know, and then formulate specific questions

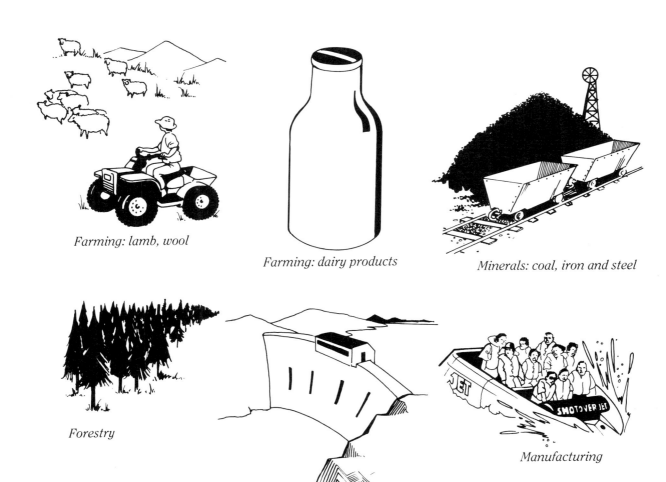

Farming: lamb, wool

Farming: dairy products

Minerals: coal, iron and steel

Forestry

Power

Manufacturing

which will help to provide this knowledge. If possible, tape-record such an interview, both for reference purposes and also for posterity: the recording may well be a useful archive for other children in the future.

Try to make any recording arrangements as unobtrusive as possible, since large microphones are often off-putting for inexperienced speakers. A more appropriate piece of equipment would be a small recorder with a built-in microphone or a dictating machine, which can be located close to the speaker (to ensure clarity of reproduction) without inhibiting him or her. Be sure that you are using a tape of sufficient duration: C90 audio cassettes provide 45 minutes of recording time per side; with dictating machines, choose the slower speed (if available) in order to maximise recording time on a half-hour microcassette. Faults on the original recording can, of course, be edited out if you have a two-cassette-deck machine or two separate decks with suitable connecting cables, thus providing a well-structured and tightly paced tape for your New Zealand archive. Microcassettes can also be edited onto standard audio cassettes with the appropriate equipment and leads: consult any reputable local electronics or record store.

HISTORY

Activity 14: The Polynesian navigators
Find out more in general terms about Polynesian navigators. These were the first people to discover and explore the islands of New Zealand. Children will no doubt enjoy researching the forms of vessel used by these early explorers.

Background information
The Polynesian islanders were the first known people in the world to use simple maps for navigation. These consisted of an 'ocean' (the Pacific) constructed from cane and twigs, tied together with reeds; appropriate objects such as shells were tied in place to represent islands. The Polynesians sailed around the Pacific in simple craft such as outrigger canoes.

Activity 15: Tasman's voyage of discovery
Read about Abel Tasman's voyage of discovery. With two ships from the Dutch East India Company, Tasman sighted the west side of New Zealand's South Island in 1642. He and his crew travelled up the west coast of the country, before sailing on to the mid-Pacific where he discovered some of the islands in the Tonga and Fiji groups before returning to Java. Tasman wrongly believed that New Zealand was part of a 'Great South Land' which dominated that part of the Pacific.

Activity 16: The voyages of Captain Cook
A Find out more about the life and journeys of Captain James Cook, and suggest that the children draw maps plotting the route of his voyage in 1769–70.

Background information
In October 1769 Captain Cook sighted the North Island of New Zealand and anchored in a place called Poverty Bay, near what is now called Gisborne. From there, Cook sailed south to Cape Turnagain, then back north to Mercury Bay. He rounded North Cape, headed south, navigated Cook Strait and went around South Island, thus demonstrating the status of New Zealand as a pair of islands, not attached to any 'Great South Land' continent. After this first circumnavigation, Cook returned several times to New Zealand, twice in 1773, once in 1774 and again in 1777.

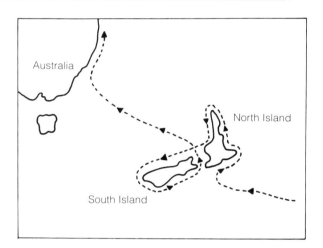

Cook's voyage 1769–1770

B Try and imagine the experiences of the first white settlers in New Zealand and let the children suggest what their relationship with the Maoris might have been like. Discuss the possible emotions of immigrants arriving in a new land ... and one already inhabited: perhaps a mixture of excitement, wonder, fear, anticipation, superiority and even dominance.

Background information
Around the years 1791–3, the first colony of white people was established in New Zealand, as a result of a sealing expedition. This was a fairly primitive camp at Dusky Sound in the south-west, which survived some 40 years, as ships plotted regular courses to North Island in search of two important commodities of the time, flax and timber. Further white encampments were established, and were notable for their harsh treatment of the native Maori people. Many of the early settlers were rogues and ruffians, there because they were nomadic whaling men, sealers or ships' deserters. One of the earliest settlements was at Korokareka, now called Russell.

Activity 17: The British Commonwealth of Nations

Discuss why New Zealand is a member of the British Commonwealth of Nations, relating this to a historical context.

Background information

Captain Cook claimed New Zealand in the name of King George III, but at the time Britain would not accept the territory. After the early days of British Colonisation, however, circumstances changed: 13 Maori chiefs petitioned for British protection from hostilities by the French, who were taking a good deal of interest in the land. In 1833 James Busby arrived in New Zealand as British Resident, setting up his headquarters at Waitangi. In 1840 William Hobson arrived to take charge of affairs, and the Treaty of Waitangi was signed. Under the terms of this treaty, a number of Maori chiefs ceded sovereignty to Britain in return for undisturbed possession of their lands, forests and fisheries. Until this time, Maori lands had regularly been annexed for little or no reward to the native people. Hobson established the administration of New Zealand in Auckland and Okiato, close to Russell, became the capital. Some 25 years later, the central administration moved to Wellington.

More is said about the Maoris elsewhere in this topic, but in the present context it should be noted that the terms of the Waitangi Treaty were hardly adhered to: the Maoris were badly treated, often being persuaded to sell their land for little or no gain, a situation which often led to much fighting. These conflicts continued from the mid-nineteenth century until 1872. The country, meanwhile, established a parliament, with provincial governments which had power to legislate on local issues. In 1875 the provincial governments were abolished, and their powers taken over by the central government in Wellington.

Many new settlers arrived as a result of the gold rush era in the 1860s and the late-nineteenth-century expansion of the meat and dairy industries. In 1907 New Zealand was granted the status of a Dominion, having acquired additional territories, including the Chatham Islands and the Cook Islands. In 1923 the country took over an area in Antarctica, Ross Dependency, which later became the site of scientific research by scientists from New Zealand and the USA. Western Samoa (now independent) came under New Zealand administration in 1919, as did the Tokelau Islands in 1925. New Zealand became independent in 1931.

As a member of the British Commonwealth, New Zealand has a Governor-General to represent the British monarch. The country is also administered by a Prime Minister and a cabinet. Traditionally, governments have worked in close collaboration with Britain, and have Maori electorate representatives. Inevitably, New Zealand has developed close economic and political links with Australia and the USA.

Activity 18: The Maori people

A Use **Copymaster 3** (Maori people) as the basis for introducing a study of the Maoris, the original inhabitants of New Zealand. The copymaster shows Maoris in traditional costume, set against a typical meeting house. Suggest that the children colour this picture, which could be used as a cover for a workbook on New Zealand or on Maori history and their way of life. Use the following background material, alongside specialist reference books, to help the pupils learn about this fascinating race. Produce a Maori wall frieze, with large paintings or collages of Maori people by their meeting houses and accompanying writing about various aspects of their culture.

Background information

The Maori people are descended from the Polynesians, well known for the skills of navigation and exploration they practised in the Pacific Ocean. The first inhabitants of New Zealand were from the central Pacific region, probably Tahiti. Their settlements on the islands spread between the years AD 500–1000. These early people were brown-skinned, peaceful hunters and gatherers, living off wild animals, fruits and nuts.

Our knowledge of these Maoris includes not only their way of life, but also their legends. One myth tells that the hero-god Maui caught a large fish, which became North Island. Another well-known hero is Kupe, who is alleged to have discovered New Zealand by sailing 3200 kilometres (2000 miles) from Tahiti in around AD 925 and returning home to tell his fellow islanders how to reach this new land. Legend tells that Kupe's wife exclaimed '*Aotearoa*' on first seeing the land of New Zealand. This means 'long white cloud', and *Aotearoa* became the Maori name for New Zealand, the 'land of the long white cloud'.

Further legends tell of the arrival of other heroes from the islands, then of the fourteenth-century 'Great Fleet' of canoes, which landed large numbers of Maori people.

Maori tribes had powerful systems of organisation. They were led by chiefs who had ultimate power, and lived in settlements of up to a thousand people. Some tribes were named after the canoes that had transported their ancestors across the Pacific. In the centre of each settlement was a meeting house, with an open space or *marae* in front of it. This space was used for dancing, singing, debating, and the passing-on of legends and family stories. Many meeting houses were elaborately decorated with carvings in traditional Maori style. Gradually, the Maoris adapted their lifestyles to the cooler climate of their new homeland. They built homes of timber and learned to weave flax into warm clothing and blankets. They also made cloaks of feathers for ceremonial occasions, a similar custom to that of the Hawaiian chiefs, as detailed in the topic on Hawaii, on page 68.

As time passed, intertribal fighting occured, and fortified villages called *pas* were built. These were set on a hill, and surrounded by trenches and a huge double fence of sharpened stakes. Once weapons such as muskets were introduced, the fighting inevitably became fiercer and thousands of Maoris were killed. The last intertribal battle was fought in 1839.

B Discuss the decline in the numbers of Maori people in the mid-nineteenth century, and ask the children to suggest reasons for this. Perhaps a diagrammatic

New Zealand

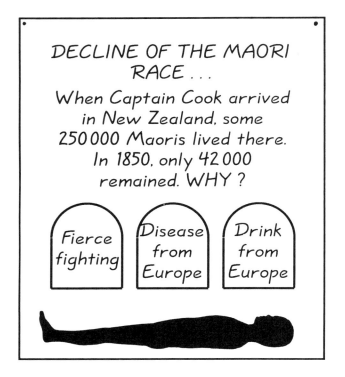

representation will help them to understand that a variety of factors influenced the fate of the Maori people at this time.

C Help the children to appreciate why the Maori race did not die out. In fact, young Maoris came together to form what is known as the Young Maori Party, and promoted the retention of traditional customs; the adoption of European skills and advances in hygiene practices also ensured the continued existence of the Maori people. Ask the children to suggest ways in which the people may have enhanced their lifestyles and improved their health as a result.

Background information

The Maori birth rate increased and general health improved. Thanks to their adoption of European skills and lifestyles, the Maoris gradually became integrated into mixed communities. Soon, prominent members of society began to establish themselves from the Maori culture, in order to play a full part in the life of the nation. By the early 1940s, New Zealand had adopted a positive policy of integration which has grown in strength to the present day: indeed, there has been a great deal of intermarriage, and the two races (Maoris and settlers) have developed together in an integrated fashion, while retaining their separate identities. Today the Maoris form a very significant part of the overall population, approximately one third.

D Discuss ways in which the Maoris have been able to retain their cultural identity as a fascinating race of people, whilst integrating with modern New Zealand society. Again, a diagrammatic wall display or similar presentation of ideas will be helpful.

E Organise a debate on whether the integration of Maori people into modern society has been successful. Some children could put forward the points of view of Maoris who may feel resentful and wish to retain their individual cultural identities. Others could represent the views of the European leaders. Clearly, with no personal experience, the children's thinking will be speculative, but this activity may help them to appreciate in general the difficulties of separate races

trying to live in harmony in the same country. Obviously, these issues must be treated with sensitivity, but such a debate could well be used as the basis for discussing the feelings of foreign nationals in our own country. From a historical point of view, it may also be possible to extend this discussion to include other groups such as the Aborigines of Australia and the Native Americans, both of whom have received similarly unfair treatment by white settlers.

ART

Activity 19: Maori art

A Research the various forms of Maori art, using specialist books and other resources. Suggest that the children make their own paintings of carvings or possibly produce some wood carvings themselves in traditional style. In the latter case, be aware of safety and the need for careful supervision at all times. The variety of carving media could include balsa wood, wax, soap or even clay.

Background information

Maori craft work became the most highly developed art form in the Pacific region. In particular, these people are noted for their development of elaborate and intricate carvings, all crafted without the use of metal tools: early implements were made of bone and greenstone. The Maoris carved boats, weapons, tools, buildings, ornaments, treasure boxes, food and drinking vessels. Common forms incorporated into the carving include one-eyed figures, humans with three-fingered hands, and warriors with protruding tongues.

B Make a wall frieze bordered by collages or painted pictures of Maori carvings. Two large columns could be constructed out of painted card as 'bookends', leaving space between them for displaying children's writing or pictures about the Maori people.

If you wish to be more adventurous, let the children use theatrical make-up and 'tattoo' their own faces or those of their friends in Maori style. The Leichner company produces a wide range of greasepaint sticks which can be obtained from theatrical costumiers or large department stores. Be sure to have an ample supply of paper tissues and cold cream or some other suitable preparation available to remove the make-up afterwards.

This activity would be a striking and appropriate means by which to lead an assembly on the Maori way of life, with the children dressed in appropriate costumes such as ceremonial cloaks. The children could tell the rest of the school some Maori legends, something of the legacy of the early people reflected in New Zealand today, and perhaps imitate other performing arts of the Maori tradition. Research, for example, the performing of the *haka*, a combination of singing, chanting and body movements. One spectacular traditional warcry *haka* can still be seen today, performed by the New Zealand international Rugby Union and Rugby League teams before the start of a game, much to the delight of the spectators, if not their match opponents!

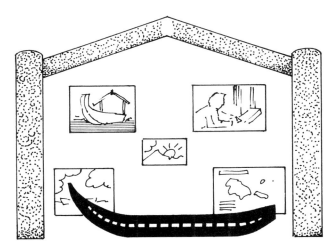

C Tell the children about the ancient art of tattooing, once practised by Maoris. Men would have elaborate designs tattooed on to their faces and other body parts, often in the form of lines, curves, spirals and whirls. Women were tattooed on their lips and chin. Children will no doubt enjoy making paintings of Maori faces with elaborate tattoo designs.

The haka, *as performed by the New Zealand All Blacks*

ENGLISH

Activity 20: Learn some Maori words
Teach the children a few words of the Maori language. A good place to start is by discussing place names and their origins: some refer to historical events, some are descriptive and others romantic and flowery. *Waikato*, for example, means 'flowing water'. *Papa-e-oia* (Palmerston North in English) means 'How beautiful it is!' One place, in the area of Hawke's Bay, has several variations on the spelling of its Maori name, one of which contains no less than 61 letters. This fascinating fact could lead to the production of a colourful and creative wall frieze. Write the Maori spelling across the top, the English meaning at the bottom, and let the children paint imaginative pictures for the space in between.

MAORI :
TeTaumataokiokingawhakatangihangaotekoauauatamateapokaiwhenua

ENGLISH :
The brow of the hill, where Tamatea who sailed all round the land played his nose flute to his lady love

SCIENCE

Activity 21: All about the kiwi

A Do a sub-topic on the life and origins of the kiwi, one of the world's most fascinating birds, and a common symbol of New Zealand. Begin by collecting pictures of kiwi (the singular and plural of this bird's name are the same), and finding out what makes them so intriguing.

Background information
Once, the kiwi could be found almost anywhere in New Zealand. Today, however, the kiwi is a rare bird, and one species is endangered. In 1812, the first kiwi skin was taken to England, and was greeted with astonishment. It was seen to be long-billed, tailless, almost wingless and roughly feathered. Some people thought the creature was a type of penguin, whilst others identified it more accurately as a flightless land bird. It is generally agreed that the kiwi is a member of the 'ratite' group of birds. These birds have no keel on their breastbone, which is the attachment point for wing muscles. Kiwi also have a particular arrangement of bones in the skull.

B Let the children paint pictures of members of the ratite family, using reference books to aid accuracy. Include the three identified species of kiwi: the great spotted, the little spotted and the brown kiwi.

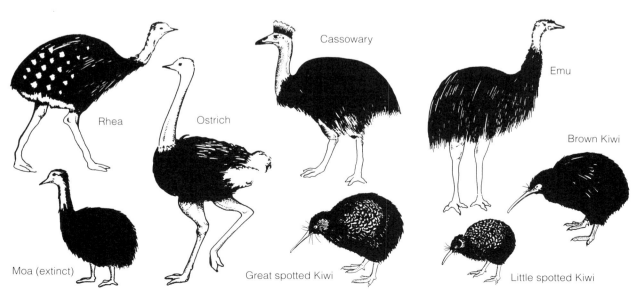

Ratites

C Use **Copymaster 4** (The kiwi family tree) to help children appreciate the evolution of and family links between ratites. Help the children to appreciate that New Zealand's isolation for millions of years is the reason why so many of its birds are flightless. Living on these isolated islands, the birds were well protected from predatory mammals, since New Zealand's geographical position made it impossible for such beasts to spread from other continents in the world. Without this threat, the ratites had no need to fly from danger and so, with inactivity, lost the use of their wings.

Let the children colour the birds in the family tree and discuss this diagram

Background information
The ratites are the only surviving descendants of the 'ancient' birds. All other living birds, shown on the left-hand branch of the tree, are descendants of 'modern' birds. Children interested in scientific precision will be interest to know that the two types of birds are distinguished by the palates in their mouths. The ratites have a double palate, whilst all other birds have a single palate. Most scientists believe that relatives of the kiwi shared a common ancestor living on the great southern continent of Gondwana which broke up tens of millions of years ago. This family has been flightless for a long time, probably around 80 million years.

Activity 22: Evolution
Introduce the word evolution, and talk about how birds can become flightless and adapt to life on the ground. Let the children make their own suggestions as to how this might have come about, and discuss their ideas.

Background information
Over a period of millions of years, the ancestors of the present-day kiwi lost the ability to fly. Some birds became heavier and had stronger legs, enhancing their ability to survive by running faster and thus escaping predators; others developed longer bills and could reach further into the ground for insects. Those birds which were better fed in this way became stronger, with a greater chance of raising healthy young, so each new generation in turn improved their prospects of survival. Because a great deal of insect food is available at night, these ground birds eventually became nocturnal hunters. In this way, the characteristics and habits of the kiwi as it is known today gradually evolved.

Activity 23: Ratites in the world today
Research the location of the ratite family in the world today. Whilst it is believed that all members of this family once lived on the great continent of Gondwana, the surviving members are today distributed over several continents. Perhaps the children could make a map of the world or the Southern Hemisphere with illustrations of ratites in appropriate locations.

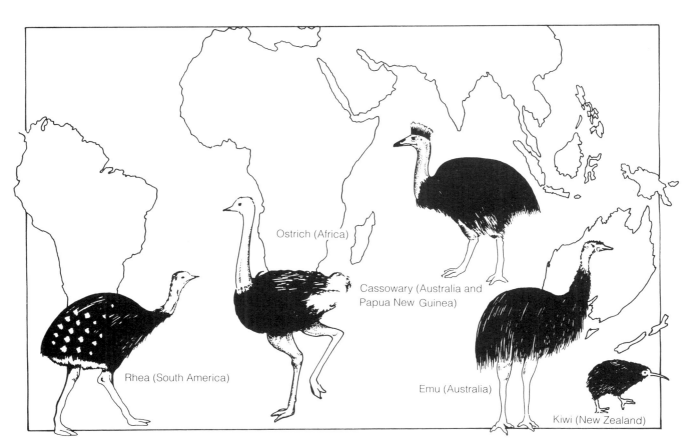

Location of ratites in the world today

New Zealand

Activity 24: Birds and flight

A Consider the question of flight, and the fact that we take this so much for granted with birds. Organise a class debate with the title 'A Bird That Doesn't Fly is an Oddity'. Let some children represent the viewpoint of the kiwi by giving all the good reasons why they don't need to fly, and others become advocates of the more typical birds who consider that kiwi are not 'real' birds at all, because they cannot fly. Some helpful facts to support this discussion are given below, and could be used as the basis for creative writing, as well as debate.

Background information
The kiwi is definitely a bird! It has feathers, lays eggs, has feet with four toes, and a light skull. Kiwi have no wings as such, no tail and are quite heavily built. Compared to flying birds, kiwi have poor eyesight. The kiwi has much smaller wing bones, and its wing feathers are concealed in the rest of the plumage. It has no 'keel' to anchor its wing muscles. The word 'ratite' derives from the Latin word meaning 'raft' or 'a boat without a keel'.

Kiwi have larger and stronger pelvic and leg bones than other birds, and so can run and hunt successfully on the ground.

B Use **Copymaster 5** (Kiwi probe hole) to help explain to the children the significance of the bird's very long bill. It can probe deep into the ground in search of insects, larvae and worms. Suggest that the children colour this picture, perhaps adding words in the space around it, detailing some of the things that kiwi eat, and then produce some additional writing about the bird's diet and food hunting strategies.

Background information
The hunting kiwi goes out during the hours of darkness. It will emerge from a burrow, and stalk through the forest, probing the ground with its bill. The kiwi is within its own territory, and will utter piercing, whistling cries to alert neighbouring kiwi of its presence. The bill will be thrust deep down into the soil in appropriate places, then twisted around and down until the whole bill is buried and the bird's face is touching the ground. It will emerge when some food is caught.

Favourite foods of the kiwi include beetles, spiders, caterpillars and other larvae, earthworms, centipedes, millipedes, fruits and berries.

Activity 25: Man hunts the kiwi

Explain to the children that in ancient times, the Maoris hunted kiwi for their feathers, for food and also for their bills which were removed and used as ornaments, for example, on a necklace. Kiwi feathers were woven into magnificent cloaks, called *kahu kiwi*, worn on ceremonial occasions. Ask the children's views on hunting birds for such purposes, and develop this activity into an opportunity for raising awareness of conservation issues, and the need to protect wildlife in general, especially endangered species. Many rituals and stories are associated with kiwi hunting: these could be researched if specialist books are available in your local library.

Background information
As the forests of the North Island are cleared for forestry and farming, animal habitats are destroyed. Today the little spotted kiwi is in danger of extinction: only very small numbers still exist, on tiny islands off the shore of North Island. The brown kiwi of the North Island is also rapidly declining in numbers. The great spotted kiwi exists only in the west of the South Island, and conservationists are concerned that this species may also decline until there is a risk of extinction. Active measures are currently being taken to protect habitats and to help the kiwi breed in captivity.

Activity 26: The kiwi emblem

Try and find examples of the use of the kiwi emblem, recognised outside New Zealand. One good example is the label on tins of 'Kiwi' shoe polish which have been imported from New Zealand, and, of course, the children may be able to discover why the word 'kiwi' is well-known to people with an interest in sport.

What sports do the New Zealand 'kiwis' play?

Activity 27: Trees and plants of New Zealand

A Pursue an in-depth study of some of the well-known native trees and plants of New Zealand. Let the children research this subject from specialist books on trees and plants of the world, then draw and write about noted species in New Zealand. Some helpful suggestions are given below as starting points for research, giving practice in the use of an index in a reference book.

B Use **Copymaster 6** (Cabbage tree), as a lead for introducing one of New Zealand's most fascinating plants, known as the cabbage tree (see below). As well as stimulating discussion and research, this copymaster can be used as a basis for the children to draw more elaborate pictures of a New Zealand landscape. Suggest that they add a background to the drawing, perhaps showing a typical New Zealand house, or other wild plants, trees and animals.

Background information
The kauri, a conifer, is one of the best known giant trees of New Zealand. It has a huge bare trunk and spreading crown, and is valuable as a timber resource. A kauri can grow up to 50 metres tall, and some surviving specimens are known to be around 1200 years old. The red pine and evergreen beeches are other native species noted for their timber.

The cabbage tree belongs to the lily family. It is the largest lily in the world, with its spiky, palm-like appearance. It grows up to 11 metres tall, and is noted as a traditional source of food for the Maori people, who would eat the top shoots and roots.

One of the best known flowering trees of New Zealand is the so-called Christmas tree or pohutukawa. This bears masses of red flowers which bloom around the Christmas period.

The New Zealand tea-tree or manuka is a very common shrub, bearing attractive white flowers.

New Zealand is noted for its many species of fern, which thrive in the forest environment. These include the silver fern, a national emblem of the country.

Finally, New Zealand has a number of other odd plants that the children will no doubt enjoy hearing about, including the Mount Cook lily, which has white flowers measuring 22 centimetres in diameter and is the world's largest buttercup; a plant called vegetable sheep, which looks from a distance like a sheep lying down; and the smallest known conifer called the pygmy pine which, when fully grown, is only around 60 centimetres high.

New Zealand: the islands

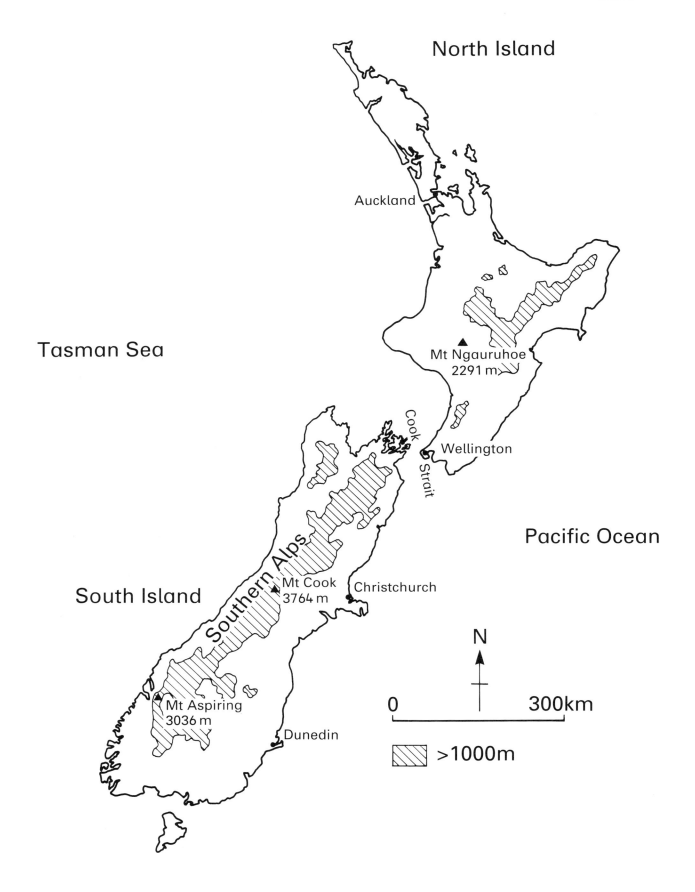

Flying the flag in the Southern Hemisphere

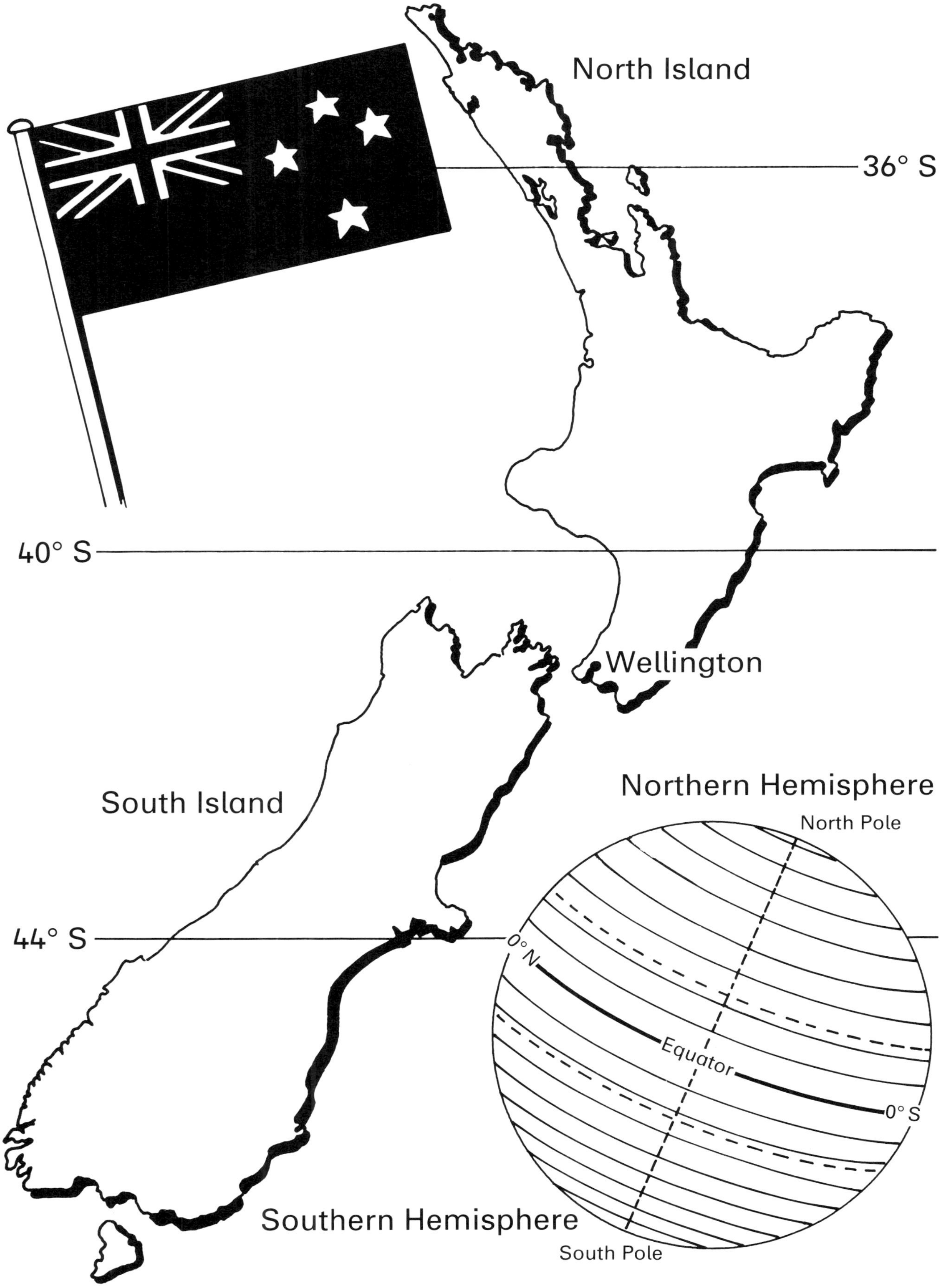

New Zealand

C2

North Island

36° S

40° S

Wellington

South Island

Northern Hemisphere
North Pole

44° S

Equator

0° N

0° S

Southern Hemisphere

South Pole

New Zealand

Maori people

The kiwi family tree

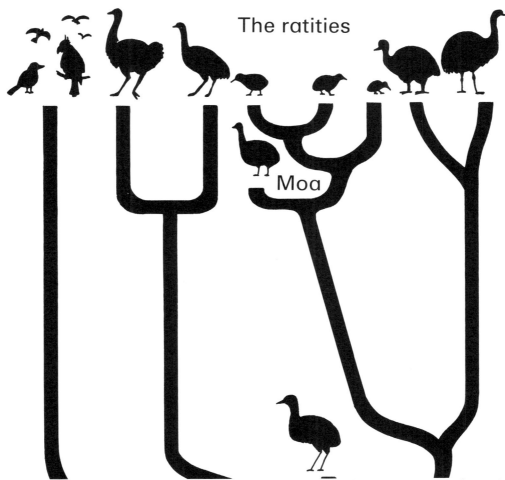

All other birds

The ratities

Moa

Palaeotis — a non-flying ancester of the ratite family

Lithornis — a flying ancester of the ratite family

Archaeopteryx — the earliest of the known birds

New Zealand

Kiwi probe hole

Cabbage tree

BRAZIL

BRAZIL cross-curricular links

Geography
- Location of Brazil in South America
- Physical regions of Brazil
- The tourist season
- Rio de Janeiro — city of contrasts
- Corcovado
- Brazilian economy
- Brasília, the national capital
- Sightseeing in Brazil

Environmental education and science
- Location of rain forests
- Layers of the Amazonian forest
- Life in the layers
- The value of rain forests
- Role of trees in the Greenhouse effect
- Debate global warming
- People of the Amazon
- Goods of the forest
- Causes and consequences of deforestation
- Woods of the forest
- The 'Great Burger Debate'
- Flooding and erosion
- Caring for forests
- A rain forest dictionary

History
- Portuguese discovery
- Early settlement patterns
- Interaction between settlers and natives
- A melting-pot culture
- Boom of the sugar trade
- Life as a slave
- The gold boom

Music
- Brazilian music - evidence of cultural past

Mathematics
- Population trends
- Rain forest destruction rates

Art
- 'Animals in Danger' frieze
- 'Save the Species' posters
- Rio carnival
- Pelé, Brazilian sporting hero

INFORMATION

The country of Brazil is in the continent of South America and is the fifth largest country in the world. All of the other countries of South America border Brazil, apart from Chile and Ecuador. For those interested in introducing facts and figures into the topic at some stage, the following may be of interest:

- Brazil is 4320 kilometres from north to south, and 4328 kilometres from west to east
- its Atlantic coastline measures 7408 kilometres
- the population of Brazil is in excess of 133 million, this being roughly half of that of all of South America.

A further interesting fact for the children to consider is that one out of every two people in Brazil is under 25 years of age.

As far as its physical geography is concerned, Brazil may be divided into five main regions: the basin of the River Amazon, the basin of the River Plate, the Guiana Highlands north of the River Amazon, and the coastal strip of land bordering the Atlantic Ocean. More detailed study of these regions will help pupils to appreciate the vastness of the country and the physical contrasts found within it.

Brazil was discovered by the Portuguese in the year 1500. The first settlement was at Salvador da Bahia and periods of trade in sugar, gold, diamonds, coffee and rubber all influenced the history and development of Brazil from that time on. Rio de Janeiro was the first capital city, but this was replaced by Brasília in 1960. Today, as in the past, Brazil is a country marked by the sharp contrast of pockets of prosperity alongside poverty and wilderness.

The plight of the tropical rain forests and the need for their conservation is an issue which frequently draws media attention to Brazil today. Teachers are encouraged to consider pursuing an in-depth sub-topic on the Amazonian rain forests, utilising background material and suggestions contained within the following pages.

GEOGRAPHY

Activity 1: Where is Brazil?

Use **Copymaster 1** (Brazil, South America), in conjunction with a globe or map of the world, to help children appreciate the enormous size of the country, as well as its location. Brazil's size (8 511 965 square kilometres) is nearly half that of South America as a whole, and almost as large as the United States of America, a fact which can be explained, but may be distorted by map projections. If possible, try and show the children a map with a modern projection which provides a more accurate representation of the actual size of countries.

The copymaster can of course be used for a variety of purposes, for example, to introduce or reinforce basic geographical vocabulary of place such as 'continent', 'country' and 'town'. Pupils could go over the words 'South America' with a coloured pen, the word 'Brazil' in another colour, and the names of the towns of Rio de Janeiro and Brasília in yet another colour. Research from an atlas can lead to the naming (in the same colour as that used for Brazil) of the other countries of South America. As the topic progresses, any other desired information such as additional towns and rivers can be added to the copymaster. Perhaps a key could be designed and included on the sheet.

In addition, the copymaster could be used to teach or reinforce concepts of direction. Questions could be posed on work cards, as shown opposite:

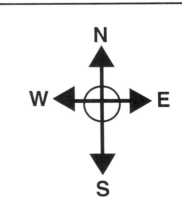

Is Peru east or west of Brazil ?

Which ocean lies east of Brazil ?

Which town is further north – Brasília or Rio de Janeiro ?

Brazil

Finally, the copymaster is useful for drawing attention to the equator, the imaginary line running around the centre of planet Earth, and its significance. The equator passes through the area of Brazil, meaning that part of the country is in the Northern Hemisphere and part of it is in the Southern Hemisphere (the greater proportion).

Activity 2: The five main zones of Brazil
Provide further reference books to supplement the following background material, and help pupils to appreciate the five main physical regions of Brazil. Explain that these are zones of particular geographical distinctions: they are not states or areas with precise government boundaries. Use **Copymaster 2** (Zones of Brazil) to highlight these on a two-dimensional map. This copymaster will help to reinforce the concept of the shape of the country of Brazil, and the relative location of key features in its physical geography.

Suggest that the children shade the rivers in blue, mountainous zones in brown and the coastal strip in green, bearing in mind that the boundaries will be very approximate. This should help to demonstrate the fact that the two great river basins, the Amazon and the Plate, take up around three-fifths of the area of the country. This colour coding will assist in helping younger children to appreciate that not all landscape features are the same height, and that mountains are 'high land' always raised above rivers and the sea, which are 'low'. The precision of contour lines and detailed heights above sea level need not be introduced unless considered appropriate for individuals in Key Stage 2.

Background information
The basin of the River Amazon, in northern and western regions of the country, occupies more than a third of the whole of Brazil. Rainfall is very heavy in this region and much of the basin suffers from annual floods. The region was covered by tropical rain forest, but vast areas of this forest have now been cut down. Generally, the climate is hot and humid all year round; the basin of the River Plate in the southern part of the country, on the other hand, has a cooler climate. Its land is higher and there are fewer forests.

The majority of the land in Brazil outside these two great basins is highland. North of the Amazon are the Guiana Highlands, which consist partly of desert and partly of forest land. South-east of the Amazon Basin and north-east of the River Plate Basin are the Brazilian Highlands, a flattish area some 400–900 metres high, and incorporating a number of mountain ranges.

Activity 3: The weather in Brazil
Collect together some holiday brochures on Brazil. Let the children browse through them and get a feel for the tourist trade of the country. This could lead to a discussion on the timing of the main holiday season, and the names of major resorts. Link this to a discussion on the climate of Brazil which, of course, varies from one location to another, because of the vast size of the country.

Background information
The average annual temperature in Brazil increases from south to north. The average temperature in the Amazon Basin is 27 degrees Celsius. North of the Amazon, states are warmer and drier. At the latitude of Rio de Janeiro, average temperatures are around 24–7 degrees Celsius along the coast, and 19–21 degrees Celsius in the Highlands. South of Rio de Janeiro, to the Brazilian border with Uruguay, the average temperature is around 18 degrees Celsius.

The rainy season in the south is from December to March. Rain is heavier and more constant in the Amazon Basin (some areas occasionally receive more than 2000 millimetres of rain per year), whilst north of the Amazon, irregular rainfall sometimes causes droughts.

Activity 4: Rio de Janeiro
[A] With the aid of travel brochures and other reference material, find out as much as possible about Rio de Janeiro, one of the country's key tourist centres.

Background information
For 125 years Rio de Janeiro was the capital of Brazil. It ceased to have this function on 21 April 1960, being replaced by Brasília in the remote highlands of Goiás, but remains the state capital of Guanabara, and is situated on the Atlantic Coast in Guanabara Bay. Rio de Janeiro is noted for its spectacular setting, between mountains and the sea. The best known of the rocky mountain peaks adjacent to the city are Sugar Loaf Mountain (Pão de Açúcar, 396 metres high) and the Corcovado (710 metres high). The population of Rio is over 5 million.

[B] Make a giant wall frieze of aspects of the city of Rio de Janeiro, with children perhaps working in groups to produce various segments. Consult travel brochures or specialist books on Rio or Brazil to ensure that the scene created is as authentic as possible.

Activity 5: Corcovado
[A] Use **Copymaster 3** (Corcovado) to help children find out about one of the best known landmarks of South America, indeed of the world. Suggest that they colour in this picture, and fill in the gaps in the sentences on the copymaster. Perhaps the children could add their own beams of floodlighting to their pictures.

[B] Discuss the task of erecting the statue of Christ the Redeemer on Corcovado. Let the children suggest how this colossal task might have been achieved.

Background information
Corcovado or 'hunch-backed peak' is the site of the world-famous statue of Christ the Redeemer, *Christo Redentor*. The peak is 710 metres high, and the statue a staggering 40 metres tall. It was completed in 1931 and weighs 1200 tons. Visitors can go right up to the base of the statue, either by car or road, from which a stunning view can be seen over the city and harbour. The statue is floodlit, with lighting designed by the famous inventor Marconi.

Aspects of Rio

C Include Corcovado on your wall frieze, possibly as the centre piece. Other sights to add to it might include Sugar Loaf Mountain, with its cable car linking the lower and upper sections of this peak, the high rise hotels of the city and the famous golden beaches, notably Copacabana.

D Add to the frieze by incorporating writing about the various well-known features of the city.

E Discuss why it is claimed that Brazilian people say 'God made the world in six days. The seventh he devoted to Rio.'

F For all its spectacular landmarks and environmental beauty, Rio de Janeiro is a city of great contrasts. Discuss some of the issues and problems known to be associated with Rio: high levels of street crime; homeless people living on the streets (including many children); and a huge gulf between the rich and poor of the city, with mud and cardboard shacks intermingled with luxurious hotels and apartments. It is the home of some of the richest people in the world, yet has very serious problems relating to poverty and social deprivation.

Activity 6: The economy of Brazil

Provide other resource books to enable the children to research the key aspects of Brazilian agriculture, industry and the general economy today. Perhaps sub-groups could work on specific elements, such as coffee production, mining of precious metals, trade in cocoa, sugar and forestry, so that a comprehensive class report could be produced on Brazilian exports.

Activity 7: Brasília

If possible, find pictures and maps of the present capital Brasília, a fascinating city shaped rather like an aeroplane, with the main 'body' containing the government buildings, and the 'wings' being comprised of apartment blocks. A huge artificial lake surrounds a part of this, as a backcloth to the presidential palace.

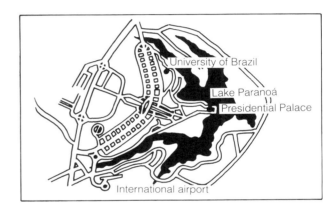

A simplified map of Brasília

The cathedral, Brasília

Brasília has been described as a living museum of modern art. Let the children make their own pictures, say, of the cathedral with its modern architectural style.

Note that suggested activities for a sub-topic on tropical rain forests are included under the heading 'Environmental education', though these could clearly be included as part of the geography activities.

Brazil

Activity 8: Plan a holiday in Brazil
Suggest that the class (in groups or as individuals) plans a holiday in Brazil. Travel agency brochures are a good place to start and the use of **Copymaster 4** (Sightseeing in Brazil) will help focus attention on some leading tourist attractions. In the first instance, suggest that the children colour in and find out more about the features depicted in the copymaster, then discuss what form their ideal holiday would take: whether it would be to visit the coast, luxuriate in hotels and sunbathe on a beach of golden sand; to trek and explore dense jungles; or to see as much as possible of this fascinating country.

The holiday could be planned in as much or as little detail as you wish (see the topic on Corfu, where the idea of planning a holiday is pursued in greater depth) although even in a simple form, this activity should help reinforce the concept that Brazil is a tremendous land of contrasts.

MATHEMATICS

Activity 9: Population trends in Brazil
A Consider population trends in Brazil. The following table provides statistics of census returns for a sample of states in the years 1960, 1970, and 1980 and should be discussed with the children. With older children, perform calculations of population increase for each state given. Suggest that the children work out whether there was a greater increase in each case between 1960 and 1970, or 1970 and 1980. (State capitals are provided so that regions can be looked up in atlases.)

Consider the location of states with relatively large increases, and those with smaller ones; ask the children to suggest reasons for this pattern. (Note that the figures in the table are in thousands.)

Background information
Brazil was once a very small country in terms of population size. From 1580 to 1640, the population of the whole area was about 50 000, alongside a million or so native Indians, and in 1700 there were around 750 000 non-indigenous people. Modern immigration began to have a substantial influence after 1850. Today, white people make up around 60 per cent of the population, 21 per cent are mixed-race, 15 per cent are afro-caribbean, and the remainder are either aboriginal Indians or Asians. In 1990 the total population was around 120 million.

State	Capital	Population (in thousands)		
		1960	1970	1980
Amazonus	Manaus	721	961	1406
Rio Grande do Norte	Natal	1157	1612	1900
Pernambuco	Recife	4137	5253	6145
Bahia	Salvador	5991	7583	9470
Minas Gerais	Belo Horizonte	9799	11 645	13 382
São Paolo	São Paolo	12 975	17 959	25 023
Rio Grande do Sul	Porto Alegre	5449	6755	7776
Goiás	Gioânia	1955	2998	3864
Espirito Santo	Vitória	1189	1618	2024
Acre	Rio Branco	160	218	302
Paraíba	João Pessua	2018	2445	2772

B Having calculated increases based on the above statistics, draw graphs to represent these pictorially.

Activity 10: Rain forests
Discuss the facts and figures associated with Amazonian rain forest destruction (relate to environmental education activities). Most children will have an idea of how large a football pitch is, so a useful way of bringing these statistics to life is to explain that an area of rain forest the size of a football pitch is destroyed at the rate of one pitch per second (every day of the year!). Today there are around 200 000 Amazonian Indians living in Brazil: in the days of discovery of the Americas, there were some 8 or 9 million.

HISTORY

Activity 11: The discovery of Brazil
A Tell the story of the discovery and early settlement of Brazil. It was discovered by the Portuguese explorer Pedro Álvares Cabral in 1500. The first settlement was established at Salvador da Bahia, and settlers came mainly from southern Portugal.

B Let the children write accounts of what those first settlers would have encountered: a beautiful land inhabited by Indians. These indigenous people belonged to a number of different tribes, and many were skilled at planting and growing crops.

Brazil

C Construct a related wall frieze, depicting a typical tribal village. If straw is available, use this for an authentic representation of thatched houses.

D Make a chart to show the interaction between Amazonian Indians and the early settlers. Note that some aspects of these interchanges were better than others!

E Discuss the seriousness of the fact that many thousands of Indians became sick and died because they had no immunity to diseases introduced by the European settlers. Soon the Portuguese lost a major part of their labour force, and workers were brought from the west coast of Africa to replace them. The richness of the Africans' culture in terms of dress, religion, food and music added a new dimension to Brazilian life.

F Pursue the above activity by helping the children to appreciate that Indians, Portuguese and later African negroes were the established racial melting pot of the growing Brazilian population, which was soon to become ever more complex. This could be represented pictorially, by way of an annotated, colourful wall display.

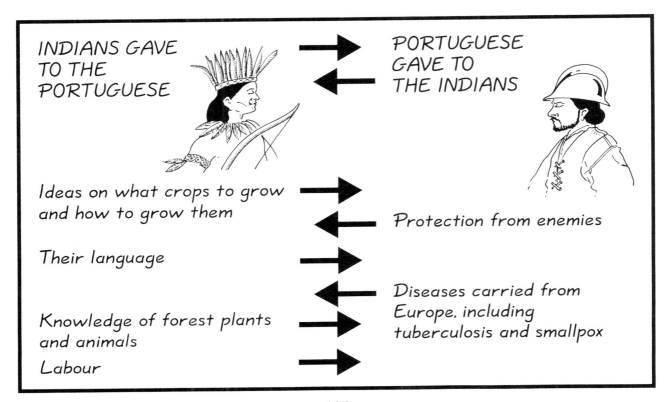

Brazil

Activity 12: Why was Brazil important to Portugal in those early days?

Discuss and find out more about the reasons for the importance of Brazil in the days of Portuguese development. Sugar was the chief crop and huge plantations were cut out of forest land on the north-east coast. The growth of the sugar trade brought wealth and the need for slaves. Read more about this issue, and suggest that the children write imaginary stories (perhaps based on actual evidence derived from other sources) about life as a black slave on a sugar plantation.

Background information

Some black slaves were much better treated than others. Indeed, many had excellent relations with their owners who marked special events in their lives by giving slaves their freedom. Freed slaves often went to live in cities in order to take advantage of an education and better themselves, hoping eventually to become professional people such as doctors and teachers.

The more poorly treated slaves often tried to run away and establish homelands or kingdoms of their own. One such kingdom was the Republic of Palmares. When Palmares was conquered by the Portuguese in 1645, its black inhabitants were killed, or recaptured and sold back into slavery.

Activity 13: Gold and the story of Brazil

Consider the impact of the discovery of gold on the history of Brazil. When the Portuguese immigrants first arrived, the central eastern part of the country was unattractive... until gold was discovered in 1698. Small settlements soon grew in both wealth and reputation, notably Ouro Preto whose riches were largely responsible for the development of Rio de Janeiro. The gold traders of Ouro Preto used Rio as their anchorage, and it soon became a world famous port. Between 1700 and 1800, the central eastern region of Brazil was responsible for the production of almost half of the world's gold supplies.

MUSIC

Activity 14: Traditional Brazilian music

Listen to some recordings of traditional Brazilian music and relate this to an understanding of the country's rich cultural past. Some of the best known Brazilian music is linked to the dances, songs and religious ceremonies of the Africans, which were passed on to the early Portuguese settlers.

ENVIRONMENTAL EDUCATION AND SCIENCE

Activity 15: The rain forests of Brazil

A Pursue a sub-topic on the rain forests of Brazil, which is an excellent way of linking the cross-curricular theme of environmental education with environmental geography and aspects of science education. Incorporate research into the importance of rain forests and issues associated with their destruction, both causes and consequences. Collect together specialist books and pictures on the subject, and begin by helping the children to understand the location of rain forests in the world, and in Brazil in particular. Prepare a large wall map of Brazil or South America, showing the outline of principal forest areas. Show the line of the equator, helping children to understand that rain forests are mostly located in the world's hot, wet, tropical areas, close to this.

Background information

The tropics are areas of the planet close to the equator, between the Tropic of Capricorn and the Tropic of Cancer. Tropical rain forests lie within this zone and on all the continents that occur within it. The world's largest rain forest is in the basin of the River Amazon in Brazil, but vast areas of it have been destroyed in recent years, making way for farmland and development zones. Rain forests have a warm, wet, humid atmosphere: a result of constant warm temperatures and very regular rainfall.

B Construct models or 3-D pictures out of coloured card and paper to demonstrate the typical arrangement of layers of trees and other plants in a rain forest. Label these to show the three principal forest zones: the canopy, the understorey and the shady undergrowth of the forest floor.

Brazil

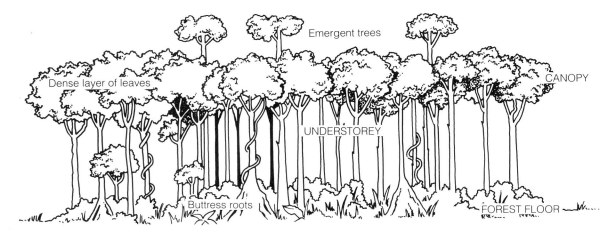

The three principal rain forest zones

Background information
The tallest trees in the rain forests are called emergents, stretching into the sky for light above the others. Below these is the canopy layer, an umbrella of tree tops which receives most of the sunlight and rain falling on the forest. A vast array of insects, brightly-coloured birds, such as macaws and toucans, tree snakes, squirrel monkeys and sloths live in the canopy.

Beneath the canopy is the understorey, a much shadier zone. Smaller trees grow here, attracting animals such as chimpanzees, gorillas, leopards and tree frogs, as well as countless other birds and insects. Many of these creatures are well camouflaged against their bushy surroundings.

The forest floor is damp, warm and humid. Shade-loving plants such as bromeliads, ferns and lichens thrive here. There is little or no soil, and the earth is covered with dead logs, fallen leaves and branches. Many insects thrive amongst the living and decomposing vegetation. Liana hang down from the tall trees to the forest floor like ropes, twisting and turning around trunks and branches. The main trees of the forest are supported by thick buttress roots.

C Use **Copymaster 5** (Life in an Amazonian rain forest) to help bring alive the layers of the forest in the children's minds. This sheet is best used alongside supplementary reference materials so that the children can colour in the life of the forest, identifying the plants, animals, birds and insects shown, and labelling them. For younger or less able children, provide a list of the answers which can be matched to the drawings (tree snake, macaw, sloth, toucan, gorilla, praying mantis, moth, chimpanzee, leopard, beetle, ants, liana, bromeliad, lichen, fern). Suggest that the children then write about the forms of life in each of the layers shown.

D Extend the above activity by making a large, colourful wall display of the layers of a forest. Use card and green paper to cut out the shapes of the trees; add collage animals, birds and insects, and other plants of the forest floor. Length of string or thin rope will make splendid 3-D lianas. Let the children research forest life for this task, thus extending the range of life shown in Copymaster 5 — the list of possibilities is very extensive. Perhaps the class could be divided into three groups, with each one researching and making one of the three layers. Add a collage sun above the forest, as a reminder of the critical role of the sun in determining conditions in each of the layers.

E Discuss reasons why the Amazonian (and other) forests are so valuable in our world. Let the children suggest reasons for their importance, which will no doubt focus upon the importance of trees as suppliers of wood and as homes for wildlife. Extend this basic understanding by helping children to appreciate less obvious contributions of forests to the quality of our planet, notably helping to keep the balance between carbon dioxide and oxygen in the air. This can be represented in diagrammatic form: sentences could be written out, as shown below, and used to annotate paintings of trees or forests.

Brazil

Activity 16: The greenhouse effect
Extend this activity into a discussion and further investigation of the greenhouse effect. Again, this can be explained well in diagrammatic form:

Whilst we cannot see it, carbon dioxide does the same job as glass in a greenhouse. It traps heat inside the atmosphere ... and the Earth becomes warmer.

Activity 17: Global warming

A Organise a class debate to consider the issue of global warming. Without hearing of the serious problems this may cause (such as melting of the polar ice-caps and a subsequent rise in sea levels, together with changing weather patterns and more serious storms), children may think that the prospect of a general rise in temperature may not be such a bad thing.

B Consider the importance of the Amazonian forests from the point of view of the native people. Whilst the majority of children probably associate trees with wildlife, they may not appreciate the human dimension of forest life. Suggest that they imagine themselves as being indigenous forest people and consider what lifestyle they may have. What would they eat, wear and build homes from? Such empathy will help the children to appreciate the key concept that people of the Amazon area take everything they need from the forest, but do not harm or destroy it. Make collages of Amazonian people, annotated with examples of their needs and explanations of how these are met.

Activity 18: Rain forest wood

A Set up a quiz to establish an understanding of the tremendous importance of tropical rain forests in providing a vast range of goods, valuable to people around the world. Draw, or cut from magazines, pictures of the goods shown over the page.

Ask the children to guess and then research the answer to the question 'Which of these goods come from rain forests?' The answer is, or course, all of them. The pictures, perhaps with additions provided by the children, can then be used to assemble a wall display on 'Forests of Value'.

B In this way the children will appreciate that the Amazonian forests are of very great value for many reasons, and that their destruction causes serious problems. Progress to an analysis of the causes and consequences of forest destruction (by burning or cutting down vast areas) with the use of **Copymaster 6** (Rain forest destruction: causes and consequences). In the first instance, suggest that the children read the captions, with help if necessary, and colour in the illustrations. Then ask the children to decide which of the statements are *causes* and which are *consequences*: this analysis will develop a valuable skill in its own right, that of being able to assess evidence and think through sequences of cause and effect.

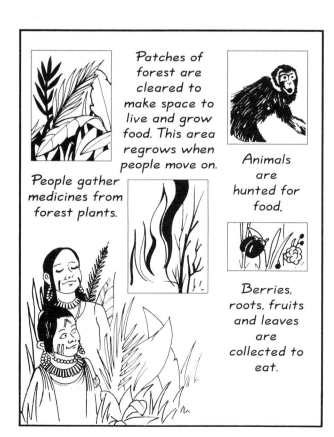

The Amazonian people take what they need from the forest but do not destroy it

Which of these goods come from rain forests?

C Discuss each of the statements shown in Copymaster 6, considering who benefits and who loses. For some of the illustrations, there are clearly gains and losses for various interested parties; for others (e.g. the build-up of carbon dioxide) no obvious gain to any party can be identified. Help the children to appreciate that, on balance, the destruction of the Amazonian forest area causes more harm (indeed, irreversible, long-term damage) to our world then good.

D Investigate the various sorts of wood, such as Brazilian mahogany and teak, that are derived from rain forest trees. Find out what these woods are typically used for and why they are so valuable. This activity should lead to an appreciation of the difference between hardwoods and softwoods, their relative value and durability.

Activity 19: 'The Great Burger Debate'
Organise 'The Great Burger Debate'. On one side, let the children argue for the need for cattle ranching and the production of beef and, on the other side, the need to prevent areas of forest being cleared for ranching purposes. This activity should also help children appreciate that environmental issues such as forest destruction are very complex — there are many interested parties, each with their own viewpoint.

Activity 20: More about forest destruction
Ask children to write stories entitled 'The Day the Flood Came', based on an understanding of scientific ideas and principles related to forest destruction. First, discuss the ways in which water is retained by a forest: trees and plants soak up water; moisture given off by leaves forms clouds above the forest; rain falls and is absorbed once more; and the cycle goes on. If trees are removed, however, their roots no longer take up vast quantities of water, there is nothing left to hold soil and water in place, and catastrophic erosion and flooding results.

Activity 21: Who cares for trees?
Find out as much as possible about who cares for trees. Many organisations, individuals and companies have taken action to raise money for projects aimed at saving the Amazonian forest and its people. Discuss action plans which are working: in some places, for example, sections of forest are protected, which means that the trees cannot be cut down. In others, special zones have been created for the preservation of particular animal species, such as the jaguar.

Activity 22: A dictionary of the Amazon forest
Research and compile a class 'Dictionary of the Amazon Forest', with illustrated entries for new words the children come across, in association with this part of their topic. Entries may range from specific animal and plant species, to native people such as the Yanomami Indians, and general rain forest vocabulary such as 'canopy', 'understorey', 'atmosphere', 'extinct', 'hardwood', and so on. Display this dictionary alongside one of the suggested wall friezes on forest life or endangered species (see also art activities).

Pages from a 'Dictionary of the Amazon Forest'

ART

Activity 23: Animals in danger

A Make an 'Animals in Danger' frieze to supplement the activities suggested under the heading of environmental education. Research which species are in danger of extinction, as a result of the destruction of the Amazonian rain forest, and create large collage pictures of these species, set against a forest background.

B Make posters of Amazonian animals close to extinction, drawing attention to the specific needs of particular Brazilian species.

Activity 24: The Rio Carnival

Read and look at pictures about the world famous Rio Carnival, held annually during February in Rio de Janeiro. Once again, this would make a good subject for a colourful wall frieze, with the carnival procession set against a backcloth of Corcovado and Sugar Loaf.

Activity 25: What else is Brazil famous for?

Ask the children to find out more about Brazil and its influence on the world, perhaps in the fields of music, the arts and sport. Few soccer fans, for example, will not have heard of Pelé, the Brazilian football hero, whilst the influence of Juan Carlos Jobim and the bossa nova may interest children in hearing other pieces of Brazilian music. If possible, let the class experience Brazilian music or, perhaps, watch tapes of the national football team in past World Cup tournaments. The latter activity, for example, could stimulate some colourful paintings of sporting action.

Brazil, South America

Zones of Brazil

Corcovado

Brazil — C3

1 The statue of C _ _ _ _ _ the R _ _ _ _ _ _ r is at the top of Corcovado.
2 From the top, views can be seen of the city of R _ _ de J _ _ _ _ _ _.
3 The beautiful statue is floodlit. Lighting was designed by M _ _ _ _ _ _.

Brazil

Sightseeing in Brazil

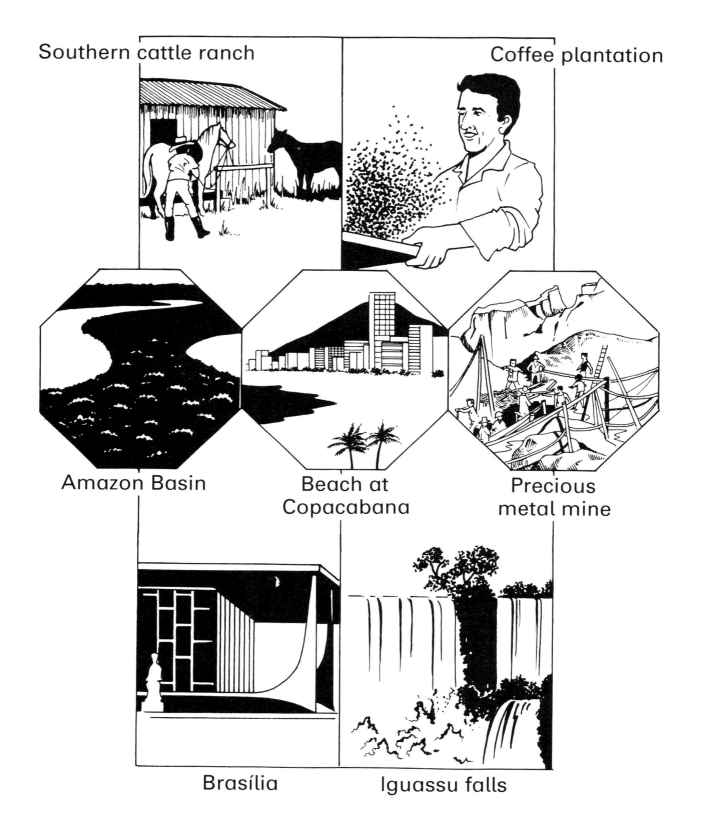

Life in an Amazonian rain forest

Canopy

Understorey

Forest floor

Brazil

Rain forest destruction: causes and consequences

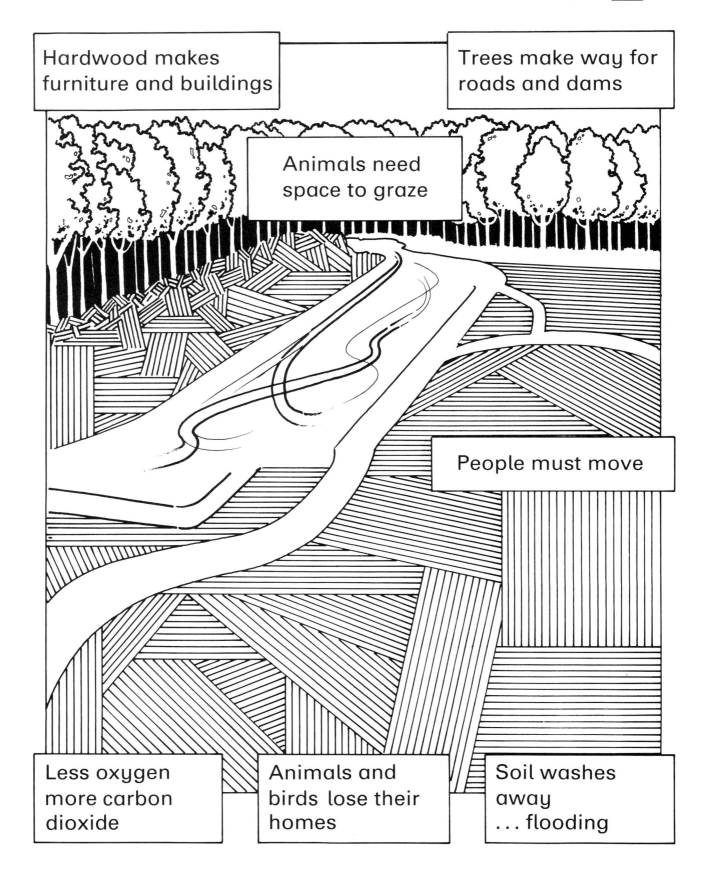

EGYPT

EGYPT cross-curricular links

Geography
- Location of Egypt
- Climate and weather
- Population trends
- People of the country
- Cairo: capital city
- Tourist guide to Cairo
- Tour of Cairo
- Towns of Egypt
- The Aswan Dam
- The River Nile
- The Nile Valley
- Industries of Egypt
- Temple plans
- Pyramid plans
- The Bedhouin people
- Varying landscapes
- Transport
- Egypt fact file

History
- An ancient civilisation
- The early settlers
- Ancient farming practices
- Daily life in ancient times
- Time line of key events
- The Pharaohs
- Pharaoh's symbols of power
- Life after death

English
- Tutankhamun debate
- Pyramid dictionary
- Hieroglyphics
- Autobiographical accounts
- Tourist tales
- Arabic language

Mathematics
- Count like ancient Egyptians
- Arabic numerals

Science
- Native wildlife
- Animals in danger

RE
- Biblical stories
- Ancient Egyptian worship
- Religion today: Islam

Art
- Pyramid models
- City street scenes
- Make mummies
- Death mask of Tutankhamun
- Print or sew hieroglyphics
- Artistic legacy
- Paint landmarks

Egypt

INTRODUCTION

The country of Egypt, situated in the north-east of the continent of Africa, is a land of tremendous contrasts, in particular between the old and the new. The ancient Egyptians were amongst the earliest civilised people to live on our planet, and the temples, tombs, pyramids and treasures deriving from their times provide an endless source of fascination for visitors to the country and those studying it from secondary resource materials. There is no doubt that aspects of the ancient Egyptian way of life had a great influence upon later civilisations, and they provide us with a wealth of material for historical studies today.

In the 1990s Egypt is a country of dramatic development and rapidly increasing population. Cairo, the capital, is the largest city in modern Africa, with its skyscraper buildings, busy streets and bustling shopping centres. The contrast between old and new, the developed and the undeveloped, is reflected in many aspects of the Egyptian way of life, for example in agriculture, which is the largest employer of labour in the country today. Many farms still depend on traditional methods, although new technology has been introduced in some rural places. A second major contrast exists between desert and fertile land. Most of Egypt is desert and bare hills with sparse population. 95 per cent of the country's people live in the delta of the River Nile and the river's narrow band of fertile land which runs alongside its banks.

Egypt's present-day income derives from a number of sources and enterprises, and tourism is an ever-expanding element of the economy. Thousands of visitors each year flock to see Cairo, the River Nile, Aswan and the wonderful sights and artefacts which have existed since ancient times.

GEOGRAPHY

Activity 1: Where is Egypt?
Begin by helping children to locate Egypt as a country within the African continent. Use globes, atlases and two-dimensional maps of the world to locate first Africa, then Egypt within it. Next, introduce the information provided on **Copymaster 1** (Egypt). This shows the outline of the country, lying south of the Mediterranean Sea, as well as the Red Sea, the River Nile, the position of Cairo and the names of the neighbouring lands. Suggest that the children colour the seas in blue, the dot for Cairo in red and neighbouring borders in brown, thus familiarising themselves with some of the key geographical features of the area. This map outline can be put to a variety of further uses. For example, other place names or geographical features can be added at any stage.

Activity 2: Temperature
Begin a study of the climate of Egypt by making graphs of temperature statistics in three of the key towns and comparing them. **Copymaster 2** (Town temperatures) provides a good basis for this activity. The copymaster shows the average monthly temperature of Aswan throughout a typical year. Provide statistics of other towns (e.g. Alexandria and Cairo shown in the following table) for children to plot on the copymaster. When the graphs are complete, look up the positions of Cairo, Aswan and Alexandria in an atlas or on a globe. Suggest why the temperature statistics vary between these towns, and why Aswan is so much hotter than Cairo and Alexandria.

Background information

Average monthly temperatures (°C)		
	Alexandria	Cairo
January	18	19
February	19	21
March	21	23
April	23	28
May	27	33
June	28	34
July	30	35
August	31	34
September	29	33
October	28	30
November	25	25
December	21	21

Activity 3: Weather in Egypt
Consult reference materials to find out about other aspects of the weather of the country, helping children to appreciate that most of Egypt is desert land.

Background information
In Egypt it seldom rains. Cairo has some rain in January and February, and Alexandria from November through to February. Most days, everywhere is warm and sunny, and so the weather is very predictable. From time to time a 'khamsin' occurs. This is a hot wind which blows for around 50 days in March, April and May. The desert sand is picked up and distributed over the country, resulting in cloudy skies.

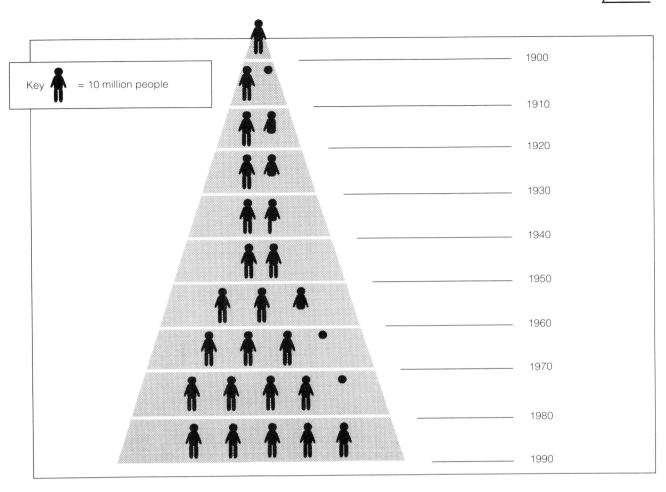

Activity 4: Population trends
Consider the impact of the very rapidly increasing population of Egypt, which is growing at the rate of about a million people a year. Make population increase charts based on the idea above, with annotations or illustrations giving reasons why the population is increasing at such a great rate (e.g. much better health care in recent years, fewer infant deaths, better food production and distribution).

Activity 5: Population size
Use the above data to calculate the present-day approximate population of the country and to make estimates for past decades. This will help the children to appreciate the great increases that have taken place in recent years.

Activity 6: The people
Consult reference materials to find out more about the distribution of the Egyptian population and the main activities in which the people are engaged. Use **Copymaster 3** (People of Egypt today) as the basis for discussion and for stimulating writing and further research. The copymaster shows a number of people as they may be seen in present-day Egypt, together with key words to stimulate discussion and further research. Ask the children to colour the people authentically after their research.

Background information
More than 95 per cent of the present population of 50 million live in the areas of the Nile Delta and the fertile strip that borders the river. 80 per cent of the country's population is made up of farming people known as the *fellahin*.

The farmer, a *fellah*, usually ploughs with a traditional yoke, attached to buffalo or oxen, and the traditional plough itself, made from long tree trunks with iron-shod ends (only the rich can afford modern equipment). The *fellah* wears a traditional robe of white or pale, striped cotton. Several crops are produced in the fields each year, including maize, which is the most important food crop, and cotton, which is also grown in substantial quantities.

The women of the *fellahin* can often be seen washing laundry on the banks of the river. Young women wear brightly coloured clothes, often in shades of orange and red. Older women usually wear black.

In complete contrast to the urban scene, around 12 million people live in the modern city of Cairo (see activities below), comprised of young and old, men and women, rich and poor. The poverty stricken intermingle with the wealthy, educated business folk and professionals in the city's exciting cosmopolitan atmosphere.

Activity 7: Cairo
Cairo, with its population of 12 million, is the largest city in the Arab world. Use **Copymaster 4** (Cairo) to give practice in skills of map reading and to help children appreciate the siting of the city on the River Nile.

The city map on the copymaster has been simplified to show some of the main streets and features. Devise a set of questions for the children to answer, for example 'Which bridge would you cross when travelling from Giza to Roda Island (*Geziret er Roda*)?' Children can find tourist guides to Cairo, research the details and background of other features shown and add their own features to the map, devising appropriate symbols if necessary.

Background information
The original capital of the Old Kingdom of the Pharaohs (see page 124) in Egypt was at Memphis, 20 kilometres south of Cairo. It was not until the seventh century, when Arab conquerors arrived in the land, that Cairo developed into the chief city. As it grew, thousands of hectares of fertile farmland adjacent to the River Nile were given over for housing development. In the past two decades a great expansion of the city has occurred, as the population of Egypt has greatly increased.

Today Cairo is a crowded, bustling, cosmopolitan city, with skyscrapers, hectic main streets and various bridges linking the mainland with the two key islands, Gezira and Roda. It is a city of great contrasts: ancient mosques mingle with ultra-modern architecture; rich blend with the poor; business people with street vendors. Many women are seen in the streets wearing Western dress, others wear robes and veils. Men may be clad in business suits, or long cotton robes known as *galabias*.

Activity 8: Tourist guide to Cairo
Extend the above activity by asking the children to research some of the most interesting attractions of the city and to compile their own 'tour guides' or visitors' reference books about Cairo, to include illustrations, maps and suitable descriptions. Travel agents' brochures and published guides will be useful sources of information. Places to encourage research about include the islands of Gezira and Roda; the Egyptian Antiquities Museum, which houses treasures of the Pharaohs and includes the Tutankhamun Gallery; the Islamic Art Museum; Ibn Tulun Mosque (Cairo's oldest mosque) and Tahrir Square.

Background information
The islands of **Gezira** and **Roda** lie to the west of the heart of Cairo in the River Nile. The bustling modern city extends on to both of them, and the islands are connected to the east and west banks of the river by a series of bridges. One of the tallest buildings in the nation, Cairo Tower, is situated on Gezira Island.

Tahrir Square in the heart of the city is a focal point for modern access routes (with traffic roundabouts, the metro system and pedestrian walkways). The 'local' atmosphere is generated by pedlars and vendors who gather every day to sell their wares.

Close to Tahrir Square is the **Egyptian Antiquities Museum**, which is the home of treasures of the Pharaohs going back 5000 years. Its exhibits include the famous trappings from the tomb of Tutankhamun.

As its title suggests, Cairo's **Islamic Art Museum** provides evidence of the country's rich tradition of the art of Islam. Its collections include ceramics, prayer mats, mosque lamps, glass and fabrics.

Cairo has many mosques worthy of note and further research. The oldest is believed to be the **Ibn Tulun Mosque**, which is different from the other mosques in that it has a spiral minaret, with a winding staircase outside leading up to a gallery. The mosque was built by Ahmed Ibn Tulun, founder of the Tulunid dynasty, which ruled Egypt from 870 to 904.

Activity 9: Tour of Cairo
After maps of the city have been studied and children have familiarised themselves with some of the key landmarks, they could describe a route or walk through part of the town, written partly from a factual point of view (i.e. describing buildings, bridges, etc. seen) and partly from an imaginative point of view (i.e. describing the atmosphere, the bustling streets, characters observed, etc.).

Activity 10: Towns of Egypt
Use tourist brochures and other reference books on Egypt to locate and find out about other towns of the country. Add these to your maps on Copymaster 1. Interesting places to research include Aswan, Luxor, Alexandria and Assiut.

Background information
Alexandria, founded by Alexander the Great in 332 BC, is the largest port in Egypt, situated on the western side of the delta of the River Nile. It was a well-known trading centre under the Greek rulers who reigned up to Roman times. The city was destroyed during the fourteenth century in a series of earthquakes which caused a huge tidal wave to flood the land. Today Alexandria thrives as a port and holiday resort.

Luxor was the focus of Egyptian glory from around 2100–750 BC when the power of the land was reflected in the temples of Luxor and Karnak (see pages 122–3). Today it is a thriving tourist resort.

Aswan is situated at the southern limit of navigation on the Nile before the river's dams are encountered. It exists today as a town frequented by tourists wishing to visit the Aswan Dam, farmers and industrialists. Industries associated with the Aswan area include iron and steel, chemicals and sugar.

Assiut (Asyût) lies 380 kilometres south of Cairo in the Nile Valley, set back from the river near the foot of a mountain. It is the birthplace of President Mubarrak of Egypt.

Activity 11: The Aswan Dam
Find out more about the construction and impact of the Aswan Dam, completed in 1972. Locate the dam on a map (see page 121), add it to Copymaster 1 and write about its significance.

Background information
The Aswan Dam is 3600 metres long, 111 metres high and 40 metres wide at the top, and it serves the key function of holding back the waters of Lake Nasser. The dam is one of the largest in the world and one of the greatest engineering achievements of the century. Because water can be released in a controlled way throughout the year, the dam has had a major impact on Egyptian agriculture and the economy. It is now

possible to grow two or three crops each year on the same soil, while vast areas of new land can be irrigated, which is essential for the feeding of Egypt's dramatically increasing population. Generators are contained within the dam, so as water passes through, it drives turbines which generate electricity to supply homes and industries.

Activity 12: The River Nile
Extend the above activity by helping children to appreciate the position of Aswan and Lake Nasser in relation to the River Nile and other key settlements and features discussed in the topic. Draw maps of the river running through Egypt to show the location of these key features. The map below should be helpful. (Note that the River Nile is the longest river in the world.)

Activity 13: Impact on the river
Discuss the impact of the construction of the Aswan Dam on the surrounding area, and debate the pros and cons of a people's large-scale interference on a natural landscape. Ask the children the key question 'Can such an impact on the natural environment always be entirely positive?'

Background information
Building the dam has not been without its problems. Mud that used to flow from the lake into the Nile Valley brought a wealth of natural fertilisers to encourage the growth of crops, but this mud and its fertilisers are now held back by the dam. Thus there is now widespread use of artificial fertilisers which are believed by many to

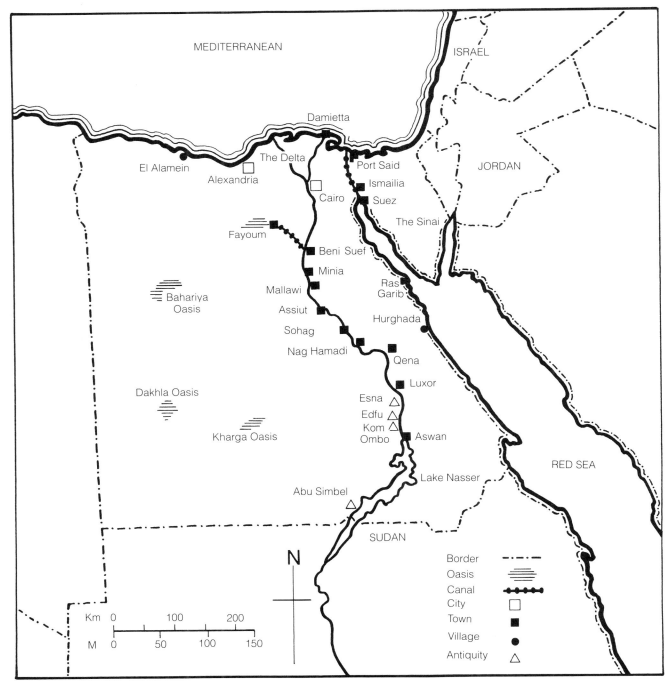

The Nile

cause environmental damage. Another problem derives from the all-year-round availability of water which, although it has many benefits, has also encouraged the spread of waterborne diseases.

Activity 14: The Nile Valley
Using information provided on the previous map, the children could write about a cruise down the River Nile, describing places and features of interest to view on the way. Again, popular tour guides are a useful source of information and pictures. Key attractions to include on the tour would be the tombs of the famous Valley of the Kings near Luxor.

Background information
The Valley of the Kings or Theban Necropolis is the site of the tombs of many of the Pharaohs. It forms a small section of the vast 'city of the dead' which covers great tracts of land on the western side of the Nile from Luxor. The Valley has hundreds of burial places, including those of nobles, court officers and members of royal families.

Activity 15: Industries today
Make an annotated frieze depicting aspects of the present-day Egyptian economy, helping children to appreciate the great difference between our images of ancient Egypt and the modern country, which is influenced by its geographical location and the world economy. A simplified map could be drawn as below, with surrounding pictures and writing depicting modern industry and its economic impact.

Activity 16: Temple plans
Give practice in the drawing and interpretation of plans by providing examples of the typical layout of Egyptian temples. Use **Copymaster 5** (Plan of an Egyptian temple) as a starting point. Talk through an interpretation of the plan with the children and ask them to colour the different key sections, and then research and write about the temple layout.

Background information
From 2100–750 BC the temples of Luxor and Karnak in the city of Thebes were the focus of Egyptian power.

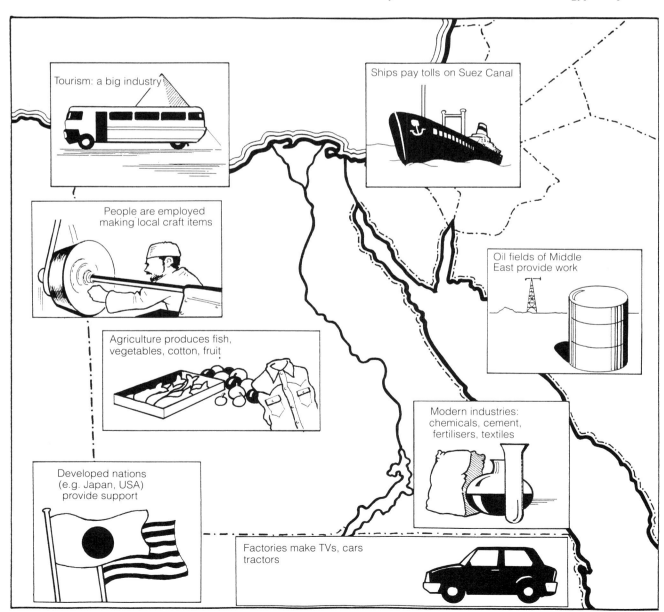

These temples represented the glory of the living while the so-called 'city of the dead' (a huge area of burial ground) lay on the west bank of the River Nile. Luxor Temple was constructed by Amenophis III (Eighteenth Dynasty) and Ramesis II (Nineteenth Dynasty) during the period 1400–1250 BC. Every year it was the site of a solemn pageant dedicated to the chief god, Amon. The largest temple of all, The Great Temple of Amon, is in Karnak. This was built and expanded over a period of 2000 years from the Middle Kingdom of the Pharaohs to Roman times. The whole is a vast area consisting of temples, chapels, sacred lakes, and walkways lined with sphinxes.

Each great temple has its own peculiarities, but essentially they all share the similar overall plan shown on Copymaster 5. At one end is a huge gateway or pylon known as the first pylon, with an open courtyard beyond. Next was another entrance or second pylon, and a second courtyard beyond that. Next was a room called the hypostyle hall, with columns supporting the grand roof. Beyond the hypostyle was another similar room or rooms, sometimes called the hall of offerings. Last came the inner sanctuary, the 'holy of holies', where the god of the temple 'lived'. Sacred rites and ceremonies were conducted by priests in this inner holy area.

Activity 17: Pyramid plans
Similar plans could be constructed to show the typical design of an Egyptian pyramid – perhaps very large ones could be created on the classroom wall. The diagram below is the plan of the Pyramid of Cheops, which will be a helpful guide.

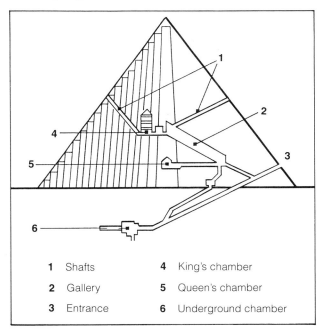

1	Shafts	4	King's chamber
2	Gallery	5	Queen's chamber
3	Entrance	6	Underground chamber

Background information
Pyramids, though uncomplicated in their basic architectural design, are some of the most amazing structures ever made on Earth. The earliest tombs, called *mastabas*, were built before the Third Dynasty. They were flat-topped and rectangular in shape. Later this idea was extended, and several were constructed on top of each other, leading to the concept of a pyramid. It is said that 100 000 men worked for 20 years to build the great Pyramid of Cheops, whose outline plan is shown opposite. This structure is the largest of the pyramids of Giza. It is 137 metres tall and made up of nearly 2.5 million blocks of stone.

Activity 18: Bedhouin – nomads of the desert
Undertake research on the nomadic Bedhouin people, who have developed lifestyles that are suited to the harsh, wilderness environment of the North African and Middle Eastern deserts, including the deserts of Egypt.

Background information
The word *bedhouin* is used to describe all nomadic Arabs. It derives from the word *badawiyin*, meaning 'people of the desert'. The Bedhouin are camel-herding people, believed to have originally come from the Arabian peninsula. They are divided into tribes, which are complex organisations made up of clans, each with their own chief or local sheikh. Staple foods of these people are traditionally milk and milk products derived from camels, cereals, wheat and rice, while fruit and vegetables are now readily obtained from markets. Traditional Bedhouin homes are tents made from camel or goat hair. Some live in semi-permanent primitive buildings in shanty towns on the desert edge, others in concrete homes in apartment blocks in towns and cities.

Activity 19: Varying landscapes
As an activity designed to help children learn about geographical features and related vocabulary, discuss the contrasting landscapes and landscape features of Egypt – sand dunes, rocky desert, flat farmland, oases, and so on. The various desert areas could be located on atlas maps, including the Libyan Desert, the Western Desert, the Eastern Desert and the Sinai.

Activity 20: Transport
Consider various forms of transport used in Egypt today – make a wall frieze to display paintings of these with accompanying writing. Use this activity to research the importance of the Suez Canal and River Nile as trading routes and the need for long-distance transport. The following should be included in your study: boats (including feluccas, dhows, large cargo ships and paddle steamers), cars, trains (main means of long-distance travel for both goods and people) and animals (the donkey is the most common form of transport to carry loads over long distances, followed by the camel).

Activity 21: Fact file
Compile an Egypt fact file on computer, to include researched statistics and perhaps key details of dates and well-known landmarks. This could then be available as a research resource, to be added to and used throughout the topic.

To start you off here is some useful information.

Background information
Population 50 million
Money Egyptian pound (£E1 = 100 piastres)
Area 241 000 square kilometres
Length north–south 1200 kilometres
Width east–west 1100 kilometres
Language Arabic

Egypt

HISTORY

Activity 22: An ancient civilisation
Explain to the children that the civilisation of ancient Egypt began some 7000 years ago on the banks of the River Nile. Consult some of the many excellent books available on ancient Egypt and study the extent of the Egyptian Empire. Copymaster 1 could be adapted for recording key places and features of the Empire.

Activity 23: The early settlers
One of the earliest civilised people on the planet came from surrounding areas to settle in the fertile Nile Valley. Discuss why the River Nile attracted such people and explain how, over a period of time, the surrounding land had become dry, barren desert, and the settlers were in need of a water supply. Find out more about how the early people gradually learned the skills of agriculture, irrigation and living in settlements. Paint pictures of early farmers and their tools and techniques.

Background information
Fertile farming land was created by the yearly flood of the Nile. By October each year the land was covered in a rich black silt, ready for ploughing with a light wooden plough pulled by cattle or men. The flood was caused by a combination of melting snow in Ethiopia and rainfall in central Africa. Planting began around November of each year when the floods had subsided.

The main crops were wheat and barley; onions, garlic, lentils, beans, figs, olives, grapes, dates and pomegranates were also grown. The Egyptians farmed a range of animals including cattle, sheep, donkeys, goats and pigs. Because the Nile flooded only once a year, general availability of water was a problem. Thus the early people developed irrigation techniques such as the *shaduf*, a device which could draw water later to be used on the land. Annual flood water was also stored in elaborate systems of canals which could be dammed when water was plentiful. When water was scarce the flood water was released through channels into the fields.

Activity 24: Ancient farming practices
Design and create a large wall frieze, showing ancient Egyptian farmers at work. Note that they never used horses on the land as these were too valuable.

Activity 25: Daily life
Suggest a series of questions for the children to research concerning the daily life and routines of the ancient people. For example: What did they eat? Did they have homes and families like ours? Did the children go to school? Did the adults work? What did they wear? Who did they worship?

Activity 26: Time line
Begin the construction of a large, wall-based, illustrated time line, showing the development of Egypt and key events in its history. The children can add to this as the historical dimension of the topic proceeds.

Background information
Around 5000 BC, the earliest farming communities were established by settlers on the banks of the Nile. By around 4000 BC some rural villages were inevitably becoming larger and more powerful than others. The leaders of these communities soon began taking control over larger and larger areas. Gradually, administrative districts of Egypt or *nomes* emerged.

There were two key kingdoms, one in the Nile Delta and one further south in the Nile Valley, but by 3118 BC the different tribes had united under the first Egyptian king, Menes, in Upper Egypt (the Nile Valley) who conquered the northern district. After this, Egypt was ruled by a series of 30 dynasties or royal families, from Menes to Alexander the Great. Other historians have identified three major eras within this period: the Old, Middle and New Kingdoms. (Old Kingdom *c.* 2664–2155 BC, Middle Kingdom *c.* 2051–1786 BC, New Kingdom *c.* 1554–1075 BC. These dates are approximate and other reference sources may give different ones.)

By the time of the Old Kingdom, Egypt had become wealthy. The capital was Memphis, and it had a Pharaoh as an all-powerful ruler. The pyramids were built at this time, reflecting the great wealth and power of the rulers. The Middle Kingdom was heralded in by Menhotep, a king of Thebes, following a period of civil war and political collapse. This was a prosperous and stable period until the authority of the Pharaohs weakened again, and around 1700 BC invaders called Hyksos attacked and dominated the north of the country. The New Kingdom was founded by Amasis,

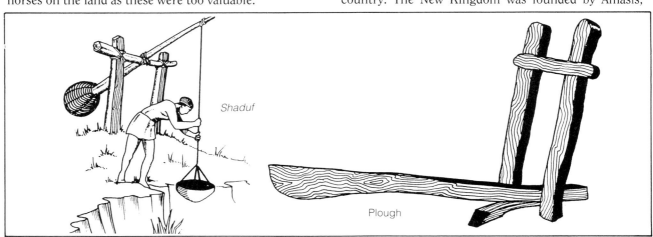
Shaduf

Plough

who headed a rebellion in Thebes. For a time this was a period of great military power, when Nubia, Syria, Palestine and parts of Mesopotamia came under Egyptian rule. Towards the end of the New Kingdom, the Pharaohs once again lost power and there was a long period of anarchy from about 760–650 BC.

Alexander the Great entered Egypt in 332 BC, and on his death Egypt again became an independent monarchy under Ptolemy, one of Alexander's generals, whose dynasty ruled for 300 years. After the Battle of Actium in 31 BC the Romans occupied Egypt and in 395 AD the country became part of the Eastern Roman Empire. Arabs invaded in 640 AD and the country gradually moved from Christianity to Islam and so became an influential member of the Muslim world. In 969 the Fatimid dynasty founded the new capital city, Cairo. In 1171 Saladin, founder of the Abbasid dynasty, became King of Egypt. In 1250 the kingdom was taken over by the Mamelukes and in 1517 Egypt fell to the Turks and became part of the Ottoman Empire.

In 1798 Napoleon entered the land beginning a French occupation which lasted only until 1801, when the Turkish influence under Mohammed Ali once again claimed dominance. He founded a dynasty which rendered the country bankrupt; Britain then acquired a protectorate over the land in 1914. In 1953 the monarchy was abolished and Egypt was declared a republic. Colonel Gamel Abdel Nasser was Prime Minister from 1954 until his death in 1970. Wars with Israel (1967, 1973) devastated the country until a period of stability began when the Camp David agreement was signed by the Israeli Prime Minister and President Sadat of Egypt in 1979.

Today Egypt's political stance might be described as 'moderate', which is why, in a problematic area of the world, it has a thriving tourist industry.

Activity 27: The Pharaohs
Discuss how the Pharaoh was viewed as a god by the people, who believed that his personal powers caused the annual flooding of the Nile. Find out and write about a Pharaoh's life – his work, duties, family and privileges. This will lead into major aspects of the historical dimension of the project – temples and tombs, which were built for the Pharaohs. Ask the children to find out what they can about Pharaohs like Akhenaten, Cheops and Ramases.

Background information
The word *pharaoh* means 'great house'. Out of respect, the Egyptians would not refer to their god-king by name, and so they used the word Pharaoh. They would explain, for example, that 'the great house' had ordered something to be done. The king had absolute power over the land and the people. He commanded the Egyptian army and was also the chief priest. As he was a god, the king could not marry an ordinary woman but only someone of royal blood: hence, many kings married their half-sister or sister.

Activity 28: Symbols of power
Use **Copymaster 6** (Tutankhamun) as the basis for discussing symbols of power attributed to the Pharaohs. Children will enjoy colouring the copymaster and writing about this famous figure. Ask them to look for signs of the Pharaoh's power shown in the copymaster and to research and write about these. Look for:

- Pyramid – the tomb of the great
- False beard – a symbol to show the Pharaoh is a god
- Buckle – the name of the Pharaoh was engraved on the belt buckle
- Crook – the Pharaoh was the shepherd of all his people
- Headdress – the vulture symbolised power over Upper Egypt, the cobra power over Lower Egypt
- Sandals – gold was used for the thong; gold toe covers were also used on mummies
- Jewellery – includes the scarab, symbol of the sun-god, giver of life.

Activity 29: Life after death
Link work on tombs and pyramids to the beliefs held by the Egyptians about life after death. Find out about the customs and practices associated with the death of a nobleman or a king. Get children to write about the work of an embalmer and draw pictures of mummies.

Background information
The ancient Egyptians adopted elaborate funeral customs and rituals to ensure that the dead entered into a continued existence (see page 129).

The mummification process took over 70 days to carry out. The embalmer would draw out the brain through the nose with a wire hook, and remove the internal organs by cutting open the left side of the body. These organs were then dried out and stored in four jars. The heart was left in place. The body was covered in natron, a form of salt, which dried it out after about 40 days. The body was then washed, anointed with perfumes and oils, and wrapped in layers of linen bandage.

ENGLISH

Activity 30: Tutankhamun debate
Organise a class debate on the investigations that took place into the tomb of Tutankhamun, the only Pharaoh who has been discovered in the wrapping, coffin and sarcophagus in which he was buried (see Copymaster 6). Debate the arguments for and against the unwrapping and study of his body.

Background information
King Tutankhamun died in mysterious circumstances when he was only 19 years old. He was buried with some 1700 items of treasure, which were discovered in 1922 by British archaeologist Howard Carter. Items include a solid gold coffin, Tutankhamun's famous mask and many pieces of jewellery.

Egypt

Activity 31: Pyramid dictionary
Write a Pyramid dictionary to explain key words associated with pyramids, such as 'shafts', 'gallery', 'king's chamber', 'queen's chamber' and 'sarcophagus'.

Activity 32: Hieroglyphics
Introduce the study of the ancient Egyptian writing called hieroglyphics, using the examples below as a starting point. Look through other reference materials showing examples, and analyse the sorts of symbols that were used. Let the children do their own hieroglyphic writing, perhaps on card or material scrolls.

Background information
One of the reasons we have learnt so much about the ancient Egyptians is because of their written records. There were over 700 hieroglyphs. Each picture sign meant the object it showed and could also mean a sound.

Activity 33: Autobiographical accounts
Ask the children to write autobiographical-style stories and accounts with titles such as 'A Day in My Life' by a modern Egyptian business person, a *fellah* or a Pharaoh.

Activity 34: Tourist tales
Ask the children to imagine that they are tourists in Egypt. Let them write about their favourite attractions or places they would most like to visit, giving reasons.

Activity 35: Arabic language
Teach the children some useful words of Arabic, the official language of Egypt. Below is a useful start to basic vocabulary, with Arabic words spelled phonetically for easy pronunciation.

English	Arabic
Yes	*Aiwa*
No	*La*
Good day	*Sa-eeda*
Please	*Menfadlak*
Thank you	*Shookrarn*
Right	*Yemeen*
Left	*Shemarn*
Money	*Feloose*
Listen	*Isma*
Street	*Sharia*
Village	*Ezba*
If God is willing (often used for 'yes')	*En sha allah*

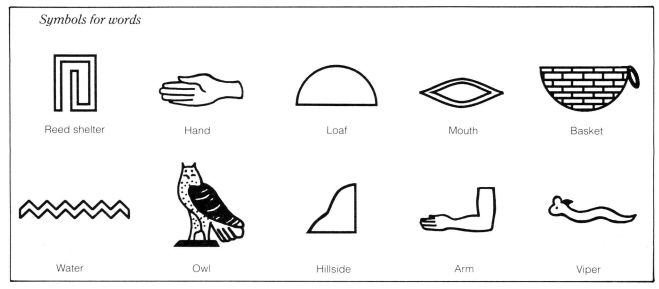

Symbols for words: Reed shelter, Hand, Loaf, Mouth, Basket, Water, Owl, Hillside, Arm, Viper

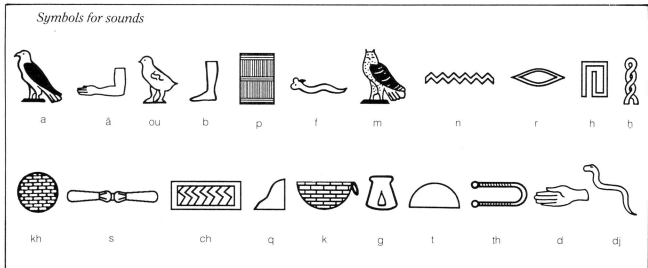

Symbols for sounds: a, â, ou, b, p, f, m, n, r, h, ḥ, kh, s, ch, q, k, g, t, th, d, dj

MATHEMATICS

Activity 36: Count like ancient Egyptians
Teach the children to count with 'historical numbers'. Explain to the children that Egyptian numbers were written from right to left. For example, 15 was written as 51 (i.e. units on the left and tens on the right). Devise calculations for the children to solve based on the code below.

Activity 37: Arabic numerals
Teach the children to count from 1–10 in Arabic numerals (see below) – do simple oral sums as a group activity.

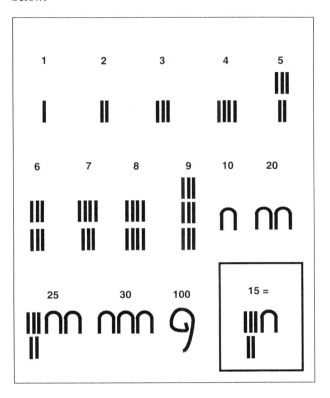

1	Wahid
2	Eckneen
3	Talata
4	Arbaa
5	Khamsa
6	Sitta
7	Sabba
8	Tamanya
9	Tessa
10	Ashra

ART

Activity 38: Pyramid models
Design, construct and paint models of the pyramids, perhaps linking this with the drawing of plans as suggested under geography Activities 16 and 17.

Activity 39: City street scenes
Make a large collage divided into two halves, the old and the new, showing a street scene from a city in the days of the Egyptian Empire (c. 1000 BC) when houses were often four or five stories high, and a street scene based on Cairo today.

Activity 40: Mummies
Make miniature mummies from papier mâché, and decorate them in traditional Egyptian style. These could be displayed surrounded by treasures made from scrap materials such as tin foil, can ring-pulls, card and string.

Activity 41: Death mask of Tutankhamum
Study pictures of the death mask of Tutankhamum and use painted card or a collage to make your own replicas of this. Use the results in a dramatic role play or display them on a wall with other materials.

Activity 41: Print or sew some hieroglyphics
Carefully cut out of polystyrene the outline shapes of some hieroglyphics or make potato printing blocks. Print the pictures on to fabric to make Egyptian-style wall hangings. Alternatively, embroider the hieroglyphics on to the material.

Activity 43: Artistic legacy
Study the legacy of art and craft from ancient Egypt. Discuss the sheer elegance and beauty of the work of the sculptors, artists and craftsmen. Consider the enormous artistic wealth of the ancient civilisation, as reflected in the discovery of the treasures of Tutankhamum. Make imitation vases, bowls and plates from clay. Display these in an 'Egyptian gallery' in your classroom, together with masks, paintings and hieroglyphic wall hangings.

Egypt

Activity 44: Landmarks
Paint pictures of some of the best known landmarks of Egypt, perhaps the Sphinx at Giza, the monument of President Nasser beside the Aswan Dam, the modern Cairo Tower or a Cairo mosque. Display these on a frieze bringing together contrasts between the old and the new.

SCIENCE

Activity 45: Animals in danger
Find pictures of Nile crocodiles and research their habits and basic needs for survival. Find out why they are virtually extinct in Egypt today.

Activity 46: Wildlife
Research aspects of the native wildlife of Egypt and, in particular, the contrast between creatures found in the Nile basin and those found in desert lands. Perhaps a large display could be made of some of the common forms of life, separated into these contrasting habitats, and explaining how desert creatures adapt to their hot, dry conditions.

The Nile

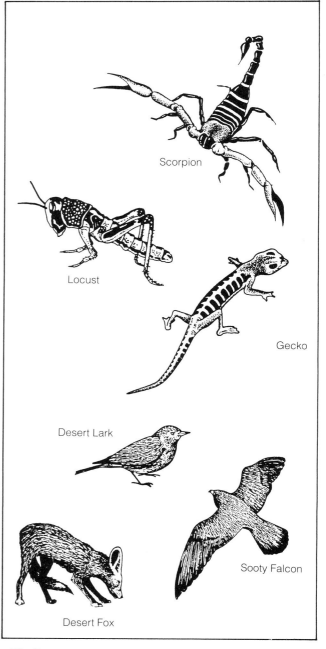

The Desert

RE

Activity 47: Biblical stories
Explore Old Testament stories with Egyptian connections. If possible, let the children see a film or performance or listen to a recording of *Joseph and the Amazing Technicolor Dreamcoat*. The tale of Moses and the ten plagues of Egypt also has great scope for drama, creative writing and artwork.

Activity 48: Ancient Egyptian worship
Find out more about the central role that religion played in early Egyptian life and the way the gods controlled all aspects of life. Most people had an altar inside their house or a chapel outside it and they regularly visited the state temples, although only the priests were allowed in the inner sanctuary. The earliest people believed that when a Pharaoh died he became a god – part of Osiris, the god of death and rebirth. Research and draw pictures of some of the gods worshipped at that time.

Background information
There were many pharaonic gods and several shared the same qualities or characteristics. Of the 'leading' gods Ra was the great sun god, who became the state god Amen-Ra. Osiris, his son, was king of Egypt until murdered by his brother Set. Osiris was later resurrected by his wife and his sister, Isis. Isis gave birth to Horus, who became lord of the earth. Osiris became god of the underworld and judge of the dead. The symbols associated with the best known deities were:

Amen-Ra	The hawk and the ram
Anubis	The jackal
Bast	The cat
Hathor	The cow
Horus	The hawk
Khnum	The ram
Mut	The vulture
Ptah	The bull
Thoth	The ibis

Activity 49: Religion today
Learn more about Islam, the religion of the country today. Explain to the children the significance of the Koran, the Muslim holy book, and of Islam's founder, Mohammed. Look at pictures of mosques and, if possible, take the children to visit one to study the main architectural features, as well as to find out about the worship which takes place there.

Egypt

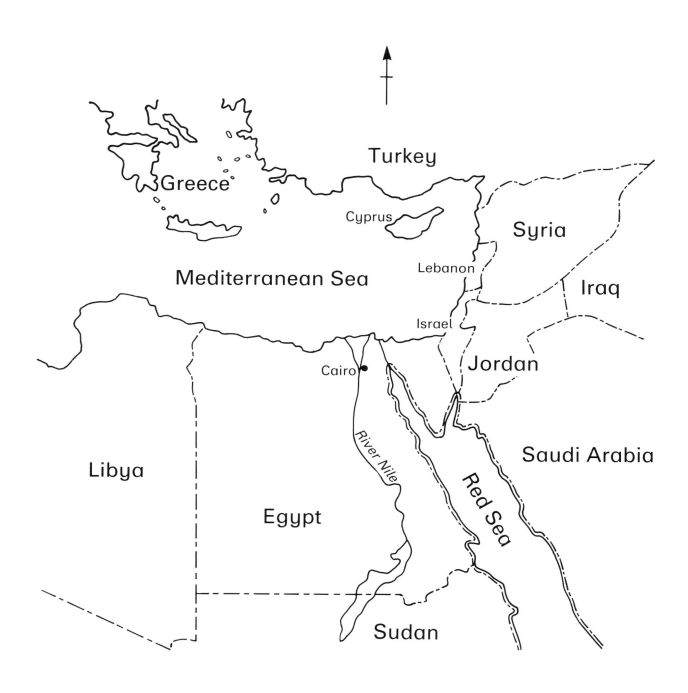

Town temperatures

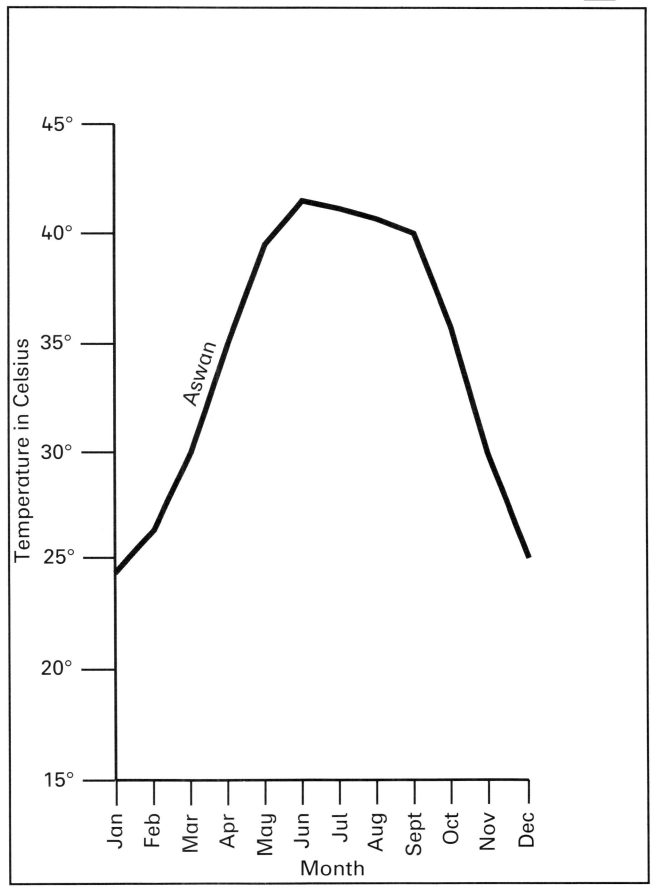

People of Egypt today

Fellahin

Woman in rural Egypt

Modern city dwellers

Cairo

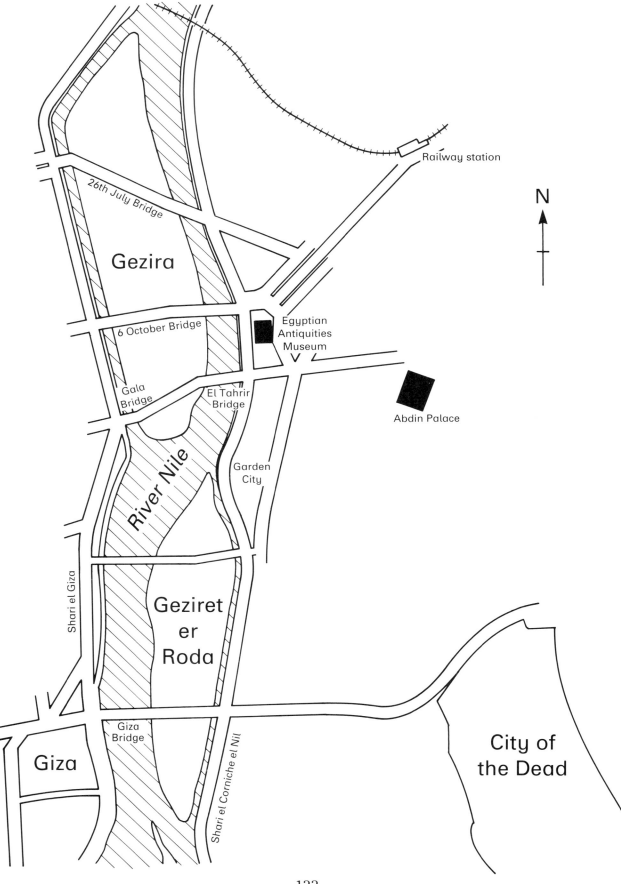

Plan of an Egyptian temple

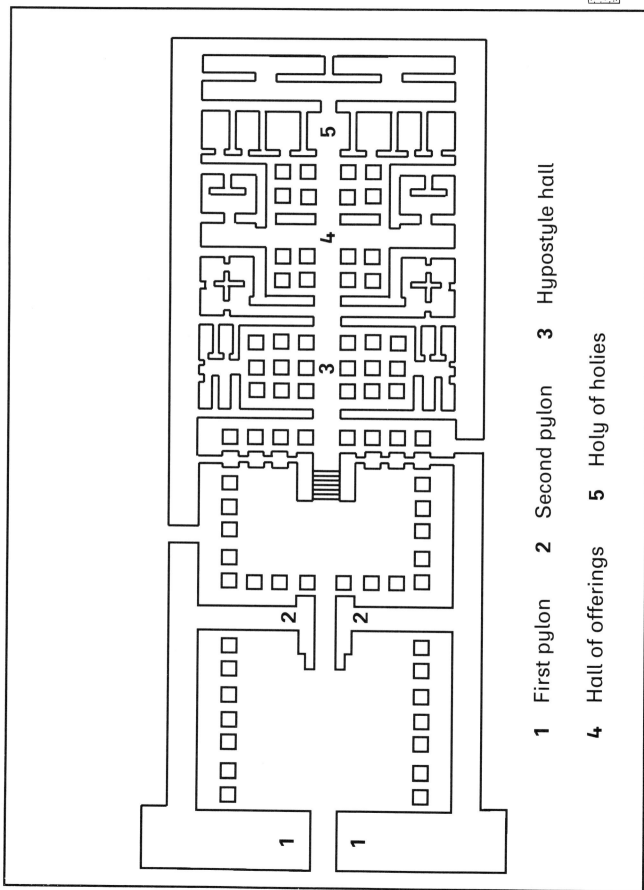

1 First pylon 2 Second pylon 3 Hypostyle hall
4 Hall of offerings 5 Holy of holies

Tutankhamun

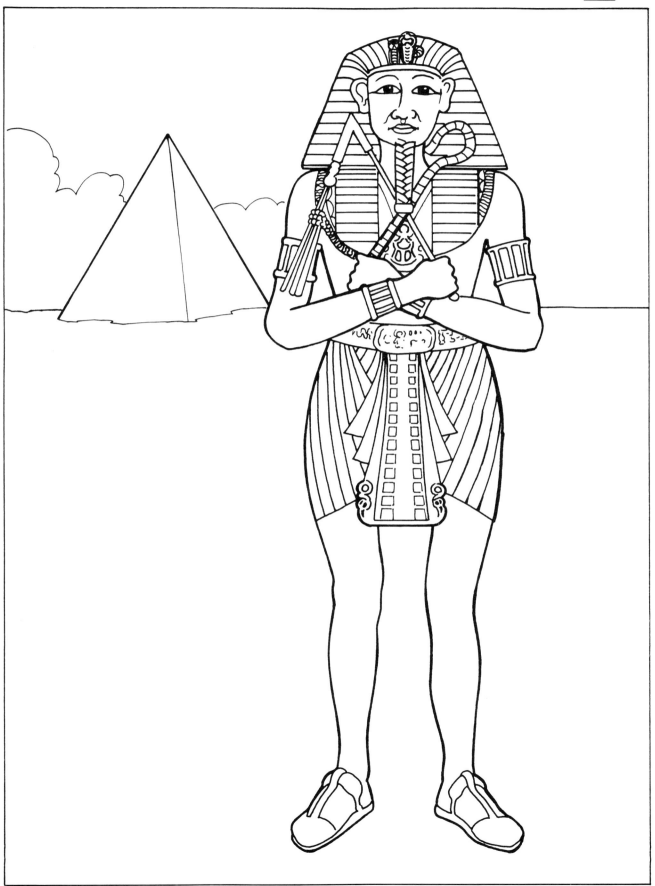

BLUEPRINTS GEOGRAPHY RESOURCE BANKS

The Blueprints series provides a wide range of carefully structured resources for both geography and history. These include Blueprints: *Geography Key Stages 1 and 2* and Blueprints: *History Key Stages 1 and 2*. For each key stage of each subject there is a teacher's resource book and a photocopiable book which together provide complete coverage of National Curriculum.

In addition the Blueprints: *Infant Geography Resource Bank* and the Blueprints: *Junior Geography Resource Bank* provide invaluable geography material, including a wealth of distant places resources. The books contain banks of photocopiable picture information, maps, templates and source material for infant and junior geography. These are topic based and cover such areas as homes, transport, food, mapping skills, landscape, weather, and different places. The sheets are designed for highly flexible use – to make up your own worksheets, for wall displays, information, cross-curricular work and assessment. Each book provides about 110 sheets and is cross-referenced to all UK curricula.

On the following two pages we have reproduced two sheets, one from each Resource Bank, which you could use to help with Distant Places work in this book.

The first sheet, 'Desert Plants and Animals', from the Infant Geography Resource Bank, can be used as a resource to support studies of desert life in Egypt, as outlined on page 123 and page 128.

The second sheet, 'Rainforest', from the Junior Geography Resource Bank, can be used to support studies of the rainforest in Brazil outlined on pages 106–109. It shows the layers of vegetation and animal life in the forest and can be used alongside Brazil Copymaster 6.

Further information about these and other Stanley Thornes Blueprints books can be obtained from the address and telephone number on the reverse of the title page.

Desert plants and animals

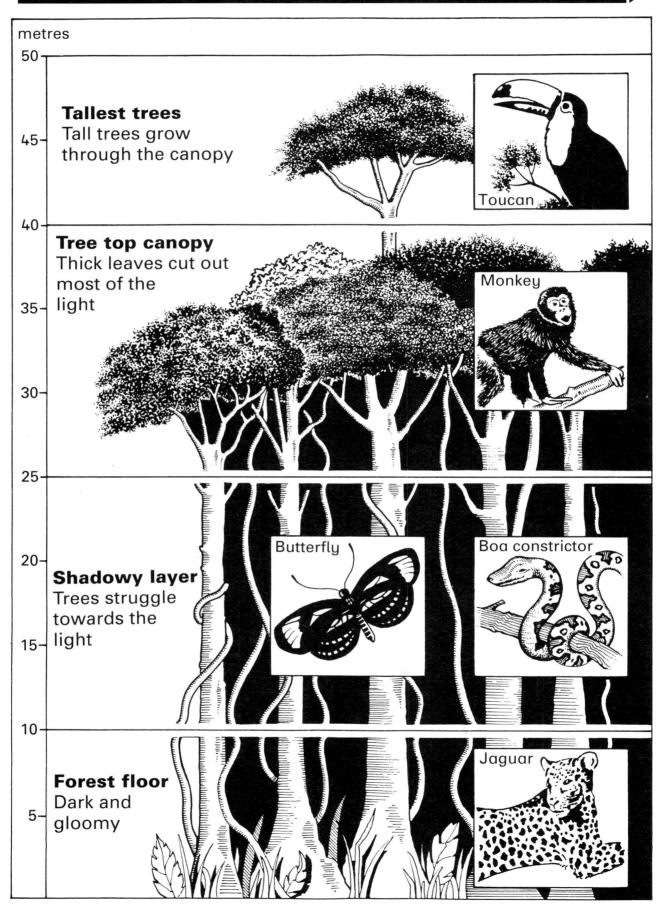